THE GIN & TONIC GARDENER

THE
GIN & TONIC
GARDENER

Confessions of a Reformed Compulsive Gardener

Janice Wells

KEY PORTER BOOKS

Library and Archives Canada Cataloguing in Publication

Wells, Janice, 1948–.
   The gin & tonic gardener : confessions of a reformed compulsive gardener / Janice Wells.

Include index.

ISBN 978-1-55470-271-8

    1. Wells, Janice, 1948- —Anecdotes.
2. Gardening—Humor. 3. Low maintenance gardening—Canada. I. Title.

SB454.W45 2010   635.9   C2009-905867-7

ONTARIO ARTS COUNCIL
CONSEIL DES ARTS DE L'ONTARIO

The publisher gratefully acknowledges the support of the Canada Council for the Arts and the Ontario Arts Council for its publishing program. We acknowledge the support of the Government of Ontario through the Ontario Media Development Corporation's Ontario Book Initiative.

We acknowledge the financial support of the Government of Canada through the Book Publishing Industry Development Program (BPIDP) for our publishing activities.

Key Porter Books Limited
Six Adelaide Street East, Tenth Floor
Toronto, Ontario
Canada M5C 1H6

www.keyporter.com

Design: Martin Gould
Electronic formatting: Jean Lightfoot Peters
Illustrations: Mel D'Souza

Printed and bound in the United States of America

10 11 12 13 14 6 5 4 3 2 1

Contents

"To my Aunt Gwen, Gwendolyn Poole Molnar,
a constant source of acceptance,
spirit and humour."

The Gin & Tonic Gardener

Introduction

WHEN MY MOTHER WAS TRYING TO BE TACTFUL, she used to call me a relaxed housekeeper. My defence was that I always thought it was more important to enjoy my children, or my friends, or whatever, than it was to be able to eat off my floors; a foolish concept, anyway. Besides, people always seem to feel at home in my home, wherever it happens to be. I have a lot of comfortable, cozy, old stuff; things that I value highly, but that don't necessarily have a high value.

And, after many years of frustration, that's the kind of garden I finally realized I wanted. Relaxed and relaxing, with nothing in it I have to coddle, or worry too much about; a garden that beckons me to enjoy it, instead of reproaching me for not working in it. A gin-and-tonic-hammock-good-book kind of garden, where nothing is forced to be neat if it doesn't want to be, and where I never feel guilty about doing absolutely nothing productive.

My grampy was a gardener, my mother was a gardener, and I've been compelled to have a garden wherever I go, even on an apartment fire escape. Elements of all of my gardens have been very nice, but none were nearly where I wanted them to be when I moved on. I've gardened professionally, studied gardening, written about gardening, and done television and radio shows about gardening. If you drove by my current house, you'd probably think I'm not a gardener anymore. But you'd be wrong. I'm a recovering compulsive gardener, and so far, I'm doing very well. I am working on a hidden courtyard garden at the back of my current house, a nineteenth-century St. John's house at the end of a row, and have great plans for the front and the narrow strip along the side once the veranda is built and the painting is done. I expect to stay here awhile.

In 1998 I began writing about my gardening experiences in a column for the *Chronicle Herald* in Halifax, Nova Scotia. I wanted the column to reflect my new philosophy that a garden should always be more about relaxation than about work.

This journal of gardening chronicles began in Stephenville, a small town on the west coast of Newfoundland.

APRIL

To Thine Own Self Be True

MY VERY FIRST HOUSE OF MY VERY OWN is a bungalow on a one-hundred-by-one-hundred-foot corner lot with blue vinyl siding that I hate. There's a large detached garage, a driveway big enough for about ten cars, and a heavy equipment business smack next door. By my back and front doors are grey wooden structures that would have been called bridges in Newfoundland years ago. They're not quite decks, even though that's what they're called now, but I like bridges better.

The growing zone is 5b. Some houses on the street have masses of old rugosa roses, and common lilacs. No such luck for me. My house has six spindly trees lined up like soldiers across the front yard, a larch, a spruce, and four grey birches. There's a bed of calendulas by the house on the driveway side, and a tangled mess of anemic musk mallow, monkshood, and New England asters choking one lanky hybrid tea rose along the front foundation. Out in the back, old railway ties enclose a raised bed about ten feet by sixty. It was probably used for vegetables by the previous owner, but now contains waist high grass and weeds, and a valiant patch of strawberry rhubarb. This is my garden. So far. I've planted nothing new. Yet.

But, along the front, I have continued the picket fence that curves over the side bank. I've also built an eight-foot version of this fence between me and the tractors next door. I've repaired the garage doors and stained them the colour of the ocean on a stormy day. I can't afford to change the siding, so I'll try to complement it. I've put up a new clothes line from a wonderful old knotty tree post, off the back bridge, levelled a spot for a stone patio, and started a compost pile out behind the garage. Last fall I started a wood pile at the end of the driveway, split and stacked four long rows of firewood, reassigned the old wooden garbage box outside the new back door to kindling duty, and stained it charcoal and stormy blue. It's all part of the outside experience of my house; my holistic garden.

In the industry this attention to structural and non-plant elements is called "hardscaping." To a gin-and-tonic gardener, all this stuff gives the garden a sense of order even if you don't shine in the planting. I have to confess I'm not big on order, but it does save you a lot of grief sometimes. For example, I have three piles of broken concrete and rocks around my house from renovation projects. I've been dreading, and of course, putting off, the heavy work of getting rid of it all. Once I finally created some order out there, inspiration struck, and now I've decided to use that debris to make the slope on the far side of the planned patio more interesting. I'll just spread it out a bit, dump some more soil on it, and plant something like snow-in-summer or Virginia creeper, maybe, for fall colour when it's rum-and-hot-chocolate time.

I finally figured out that working with what you've got instead of trying to change it is the first basic rule for minimizing stress and work in your garden. Nature usually knows what she's doing, and enhancing what she's given you makes a lot more sense than fighting it. Of course it's possible to turn a dry, rocky, clay yard into a rose garden, but you won't be relaxing much.

The next step is to make a plan. I find designing a dream garden is a lot of fun. Even if I never stick to it, I'll feel a bit more relaxed because I feel organized and in control, plus there's a comfort in knowing I'm a wonderful gardener on paper.

2
. . . .

Learn a Little, Relax a Lot

MAKING A LONG-TERM PLAN FOR YOUR GARDEN, but not feeling compelled to follow it is more serious advice than it sounds. A garden is a work in progress. Understanding that I can change my mind a dozen times doesn't contradict the fact that having a plan takes away indecision, which is one of my curses.

So here's how you make a good, non-intimidating plan, whether you're a new gardener, a weary gardener, or not even really a gardener at all, but simply someone who'd like to do something so you can hold your head up in the neighbourhood.

First of all, learn a bit. Take out a couple of library books, pick up some gardening magazines, or get them from the library too. (Even if you're not much of a reader, you can look at the pictures, and know which ones appeal to you.) Watch the gardening shows on television, talk to gardening friends or neighbours. You'll get advice on what to plant in the shade or sun, advice on budget, advice on soil, advice on tools. Take it all in, and then remember this; above all, you are the most important tool in your garden. Which, of course, can be a good thing or a bad thing, but there's no point in making plans that don't fit your lifestyle or personality.

If you're very neat, maybe globe cedars, symmetrical plantings, and a velvety lawn will appeal to you. That's okay; a little boring maybe, and definitely not relaxing. The neater and more formal a garden, the more weeds stick out like sore thumbs. Now that is not a good thing. How can you lounge around enjoying a gin and tonic and a good book if you can't ignore weeds? No, the best way to be able to relax in your garden is to make sure that you're not the only thing out there that looks relaxed. There are all kinds of wonderful plants and shrubs that can cheerfully embrace and interact with each other in a happy jumble, perfectly camouflaging any unwanteds, and perfectly content to be left alone until you're in the mood for a little interaction yourself.

I'm always in the mood in the spring and in the early fall. During the summer, however, what doesn't get done in the early morning or during the scattered evening never gets done. Oh yes, you have to do some things. There is no such thing as a no-maintenance garden, unless you pave the whole thing, and, even then, weeds will find a way through. But there are plants that are wonderfully forgiving, and won't sulk even if you go away for a few weeks. Look around your neck of the woods and notice what grows in spite of neglect. Here in Atlantic Canada, day lilies, common lilacs, and rugosa roses; even peonies can be seen still blooming in gardens abandoned so long ago that the houses have crumbled.

Flowering annuals should be the last thing you think about. Think of them as the clothing for the muscles (perennials) that surround the bones (trees and shrubs) of your garden. The most expensive designer outfit won't disguise a poor body. A garden is no different

So a good garden plan involves hardscaping first—walkways, driveways, practical utility, and play areas for your lifestyle. Then trees and shrubs planted or removed, for shade or sun, privacy or space. Perennials you can rely on year after year. Flowering annuals don't really need to be in the plan at all, because like your wardrobe, you can vary them every year.

My dream garden is full of old-fashioned perennials and roses: shamelessly untidy shrubs, climbers, and ramblers. I've done a rough sketch where I want beds. It's far too much like work to do in one season because I don't want to be at it all the time and can't afford to pay anybody. This summer I plan to finish the stone patio, plant a few shrubs, some roses, and probably succumb to a few perennials; foxgloves and delphiniums maybe, and the perennial sweet pea, before I

settle back and relax. Somewhere I have a file full of articles about old varieties of roses that I've been saving for the time when I had a garden with enough sun to keep roses happy. Now I have the garden and the sun, if only I knew what I did with the file. I'll find it, and I'll lovingly research all the wonderful new and old shrub rose varieties for hardiness and non-fussiness. I won't plant any of them where they'll look best from the street. I'll plant my garden where I can see it best just by raising my eyes from my book.

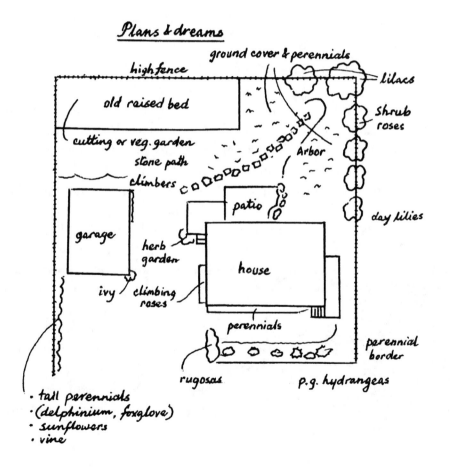

Plans & dreams

high fence

ground cover & perennials

lilacs

old raised bed

Shrub roses

cutting or veg. garden

stone path

Arbor

climbers

patio

day lilies

garage

herb garden

house

ivy   climbing roses

perennials

perennial border

rugosas

p.g. hydrangeas

· tall perennials
· (delphinium, foxglove)
· sunflowers
· vine

A Bathtub by Any Other Name

ISN'T IT AMAZING THE THINGS YOU CAN FIND when the snow melts? I mean, how could I have forgotten that I had a bathtub out behind the garage? A boring straight-sided bathtub that I took out of the bathroom last summer in favour of a lovely deep, old beauty on legs. Nobody wanted to pay ten dollars for it at my yard sale, and you know I couldn't take a perfectly good bathtub to the dump.

That tub is going to be my back door herb garden. It's not very big, but it will do just fine for my basics: dill, chives, oregano, parsley, and thyme (we all have different basics), and for a few others too.

I may have enough pine wainscotting left over from creating an indoor surround for the new old-tub to disguise the old old-tub outdoors. Or I may use wooden slabs, which are fairly easy to get in rural areas. Come to think of it, I have a bunch of slabs that I picked up last year to make window boxes for the garage. I forgot to get a "round tuit," so the window boxes didn't get made. But I see them, in my mind's eye, every time I look at the garage windows, and that's almost as good.

Anyway, I thought about sinking the tub into the ground and making a pond, but that's too ambitious for me right now. So I'll close it in somehow, creating a ledge wide enough to sit on. Then I'll use some of my rock debris as drainage, and dump in the ten huge bags of soil I got last year for the window boxes and, *voila*, a manageable little garden that I don't have to bend over backwards or frontwards for.

I don't want the top of the tub to show white over the soil line. I could make a wooden lip down around the inside, or maybe use landscape cloth. This is very much in the brainstorming stages, so I haven't worked out the finer construction points yet, except that I know I won't be hiring anyone to do this. So it may be a little rough, which makes me think maybe I should use the slabs. When you use slabs, you're obviously going after a rustic look, in which case people expect things to have a certain rough charm. (In case you don't know, slabs are the outside cut of saw logs, usually with the bark intact.) Many saw mills consider them scrap, and will gladly let you help yourself to a few. They don't last like treated lumber would, of course, but I like the look of them, and as they're either cheap or free, I also like the price of them. You could use them over pressurized lumber, or treat them, for a more permanent rustic look, or just be prepared to replace them every so many years, and don't do anything with them that involves a whole lot of putting together or taking apart. I opt for the latter.

I also know I'm not going to buy any material. If I can't do this out of salvage and recycled scrap material, I am not the daughter my mother raised. Even if I had pots of money, I can't resist the challenge.

There'll be no weeding because I will be practising intensive planting. That's a horticultural way of saying I'm going to cram so much into that tub that there won't be room for a weed to take root. In fact, maybe I'll bury a piece of that old soaker hose I know is in the garage somewhere, right in the tub, and then I won't have to think so much about watering either. Just turn it on of a morning, as I'm taking my coffee to the back bridge, or passing by with a load of clothes for the line.

Oh, I can smell the lemon balm now.

That gives me another idea! In the old old-tub I could grow aromatic herbs and thingys for my baths in the new old-tub. That would be most appropriate.

The Garden Path of Least Resistance

WELL I CHANGED MY MIND about using my old bathtub as a planter. I decided to move the remains of the winter woodpile into the garage to clear an access route for my trusty station wagon to bring rocks and stuff to my planned patio. I had some nice pieces left with a really interesting bark, juniper I think, too pretty to burn. Then I had the brainwave of rolling them over to that spot by the side door where I was going to put the bathtub, arranging them on end, side by side, and there's my planter.

It has a lovely thick, textured, reddish-brown bark, and a few well-placed nails to make sure it won't move! I filled the bottom with a wheelbarrow load of dried grass, and some "green side down" sods. I finished it off with those bags of soil I bought with good intentions last year. So far it's got only two clumps of chives and two of thyme, but looks so good it inspired me to clean up the narrow bed on the other side of the door.

This excuse for a bed was a mess of calendulas and weeds, edged with rotting boards. I pulled out the boards and everything else, rounded off the edge, and hung a couple of pieces of four-by-eight lattices on the house wall behind it. There I planted my perennial sweet pea seeds, a climbing yellow rose whose name I promptly forgot, and a few cotoneaster *Dammeri* cuttings. I think they'll get along.

This cotoneaster (caw-tawney-aster) is one of my favourite ground covers. It's a fast grower, with stems that take root wherever they touch the soil. The sturdy stems have a small dark green oval leaf that may stay green all winter, or take on a bronze hue, and a bright red berry. It's so accommodating that you can take branched pieces of it, leaves, berries and all, stick them in water, or right in wet soil, and more often than not, they'll root. Now that's my kind of plant! The ones that I've started now in Stephenville, Newfoundland, came from Sydney, Nova Scotia, via a garden in Corner Brook, Newfoundland. There's an odd pleasure in knowing the history of your plants.

The perennial sweet pea is a perfect gin-and-tonic garden flower, very unlike its fussy annual cousin. The perennial blooms only in shades of pinks and mauves, but it doesn't complain about poor soil or lack of watering. Though common in old cottage gardens in England, for some reason it's not that popular here, even though the seeds aren't hard to come by.

But back to the bathtub. Plan B is under way, much more work, but I'm feeling ambitious this week. I've dug the tub snugly into the slope on the edge of the planned stone patio area. Around the tub's back and sides I've piled all my rocks and pieces of concrete debris. The new plan is to ensconce the tub in chicken wire and then use concrete and some kind of aggregate to make it look like an old trough, catching water trickling down from the mound behind it. I know it sounds like a lot of work for a gin-and-tonic gardener, but it's really just an adult version of making mud pies, or playing blocks. The only thing technical about it is installing a small pump and hose, and how hard can that be?

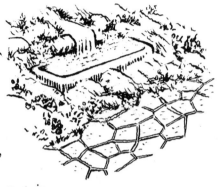

On the far side of the mound, I've put in some snow-in-summer, descendants from my Aunt Gladys's garden in Gander, both gone but not forgotten. I love this stuff, but don't put it near a lawn, or anywhere where you can't control it, because it is very invasive. I've grown it on banks where it could take over but had nowhere else to go, and it was terrific, with its silvery foliage, and masses of sweet-scented white flowers in the spring. It also looks great spilling out over rock planters. It spreads underground, but close to the surface, so an edging six inches deep will usually keep it under control, and for some reason it seems less aggressive in rock gardens than it is near lawns.

Anyway, if it does take over the mound, I just won't have to worry about planting anything else there.

Dreaming of Courtyards, Wine, and Goodbye to Grass

MY SIDE DOOR IS ACTUALLY MY FRONT DOOR, because it's the door closest to the driveway, and the one everybody, even company, uses as the entrance to my house. I thought I was doing pretty good to smarten it up by making my ingenious log-sided herb bed on one side of the door, and rejuvenating the bed along the foundation on the other side.

All that activity disturbed the gravel outside the door. There was obviously old concrete under the gravel, and I decided to get my deck broom and start sweeping. So far I've cleared an area about twelve feet by fifteen feet,, and it goes further. The concrete seems to have been spread without any separations or joints. The random cracks and dark blue stones used for aggregate give it sort of an ancient-ruin look. Of course there's a fine line between ancient ruin and old mess, but in my mind it's already a courtyard. You know, from a lemon, make lemonade.

And from dandelions, make dandelion wine. I've never made it, but I have lots of the raw ingredients in the front green stuff that passes for lawn. When we were kids, my father used to send us up the back lane with a dipper (saucepan) to pick young dandelion leaves for his supper, because my mother certainly had no dandelions in her garden. Eyeing my yellow carpet this week, he wryly observed I might as well start making wine, and I think he's right. I don't even particularly like lawn, preferring ground covers, so waging war on dandelions is far down my list of priorities this season.

I always wonder why nurseries don't promote ground covers more. Every time I see someone struggling to mow grass on a bank I want to stop and evangelize about ground covers. No matter how dry, steep, sunny, shady, or rocky the site, there's a ground cover that will be happy there. Many of them have lovely flowers, almost all have nice foliage, sometimes evergreen, and, best of all, you don't have to mow them.

Even if you're not like me, and have no desire to replace all your grass with clumping, carpeting and hummocking plants, there are still many areas where ground cover will save you a lot of grief. Why struggle to establish grass under trees, or waste valuable sipping-and-reading time, mowing, or

God forbid, hand trimming, when you could plant a ground cover that will choke out weeds, and look just fine without demanding too much attention?

There are many different kinds, with different growing and spreading habits. To me, a mixture of textures, heights, and colours of ground covers is much more attractive, and infinitely more interesting than plain old grass. Years ago, I brought some ajuga from Cape Breton to a friend in Newfoundland who had just bought a house set on a steep slope up from the road. At that time, neither of us had seen ajuga growing in Newfoundland, so she tried it on one side of her path and sodded the other side. Now one side is a rich blue carpet in June, just about the time she ties the mower on to the verandah to start maintaining the lawn side. Had she known how quickly the ajuga would fill in, she never would have sodded the other side. It would be a big job to get rid of the well established grass now, but I think I'd do it. In fact I may do that very thing, starting with my front yard. Rent a sod cutter and get rid of the works.

But now I'm getting ahead of myself and my courtyard. I have a tendency to do that, get carried away with new garden ideas. Somehow the dreaming is what I'm best at. I should be concentrating on getting my latest seed purchases in the ground: Heavenly Blue morning glory, Scarlet Runner beans and nasturtiums (which also weren't in the plan, but you have to yield to some temptation).

Remembering on Mother's Day

MY MOTHER GREW FLOWERS. In Newfoundland during the fifties, with no money for frills, growing flowers instead of vegetables said as much about my mother as it did her garden. Many cuttings, slips, and roots came from others, in the age-old tradition of gardeners. I was an adult before I learned the real names of Uncle George's geum, or Aunt Gladys's snow-in-summer.

Fertilizer was a challenge. Any spare money had to go for seeds so Mom was always on the lookout for free fertilizer. One spring she got her hands on a few buckets of caplin (smelt-like fish that roll on the beaches in early June), and had my older sister and me bury them in the beds. A garden full of yowling cats that night told her we had ignored her instructions to dig deep.

Another morning we woke up to the sight of large whitish mounds all over the garden. We had just seen the movie *The Blob* and were sure that Steve McQueen would show up any minute. Mom had read that yeast was good for the soil and had gotten her hands on a few outdated cases, which she sprinkled over the garden. Something called her away before she could dig it in. That night we had a warm misty rain, and the soil surface simply rose.

My dad got TB, and Mom found an outside job. Before she went to work in the morning, she'd either make a batch of bread or wash a load of clothes in the wringer washer, hang it out, and serve us all a hot breakfast. If it was bread day, one of us would race home at recess time to punch it down, and at lunchtime, seven pans would be ready for the oven. Through all this, her joy was her garden. I don't know where she found the time. But I do know where she found the money.

Fed and nurtured as they were, her dahlias increased at an astonishing rate, and in the spring we'd get busy, dividing, bagging and labelling roots for sale at the groceteria downtown. Ann's Orange Cactus, or Pop's Giant Red and White were soon accepted varieties in town gardens.

She loved her roses best. My favourite memory of my mom's roses is waking up just before dawn to low voices and beams of light below my bedroom window. "Now this is Ena Harkness, and of course you remember Dorothy Perkins and Jiminy Cricket. They came through the winter really well, but I'm a little worried about President Herbert Hoover." Who were these people and why was my mother whispering about them in the early dawn? Then, "Oh! Crimson Glory," and oohing and aahing over the perfume, and I knew at once, for which one of us didn't know that Crimson Glory was our mother's favourite rose? My Aunt Gladys had arrived on the early train, and they just couldn't wait for daylight to look at the roses.

When school started in September, we kept our teachers' desks well supplied with gorgeous bouquets. All the girls would flock around me, exclaiming over the colours and the scent, and I'd off-handedly toss out words like gladioli and nemesia and "scabiosa", and enjoy my moment of fame.

Later, I'd have to pay for that pride. The Newfoundland season is very short and my mother was determined to save her garden as long as possible, so out we'd go at night, armed with old bed sheets, curtains, tablecloths, and clothes pins, covering the beds. We were embarrassed to be seen doing it. Finally she'd give in to the inevitable, and we would wake up one morning to blackened dahlias and know it was time to start digging and sorting in the readiness for the spring sale of Mrs. Lewis's White Pompom and the like.

When I was fifteen, we moved to a small outport. It was windswept and rocky, but Mom started another gar-
den. Horses and sheep roamed the hills.
This was good news and bad news; Mom
had to build a fence to keep them out of
garden, but all she had to do was supply
us with a five-gallon bucket and she had all
the fertilizer she could use. This was not the
best way to make an impression as new kids in
town, but it did keep us humble.

I learned optimism from my mother. To be a flower gardener in Newfoundland you have to have to be an optimist. I learned the work ethic and the value of reusing and recycling long before we knew it was good for the planet. I learned how to keep going, but not when to give up. No matter what life throws at me, my spirit always renews itself in the spring, just like my mother's did, and I am very thankful that I am the daughter of a gardener.

My Name Is Janice and I'm a Gardenoholic

REMEMBER I SAID I WAS A RECOVERING compulsive gardener? I really thought I could garden just a little bit and keep it under control. Ha!

I was quite under control. In fact, I've been holding myself a little aloof from the garden because I've been under some subtle professional and personal pressure to move across the island to St. John's. I can't seem to say yes or no, but what's the point of having all these wonderful plans, and long-term projects if you're not sure you're going to stay put for a while. Why plant a Virginia creeper on the very corner of the fence where you're thinking of nailing up a "For Sale" sign. I actually put a sign up, just to see what would happen.

So the bathtub languished out back, another log planter on the side of the garage waited for soil, a pack of Scarlet Runner bean seeds looked at me reproachfully every time I sat at my computer.

Not only that, I've just bought an old fishing shack, right on the beach, surrounded by beach roses, peas, wild strawberries, and raspberry canes. I think that's what saved me from succumbing to the improved prospects in the city. There was a woman coming by to look at my house, and instead of being home checking for dust, I was puttering down at the shack, and thinking up an excuse for putting her off. I finally realized there was something wrong with that picture, and came home and took down the "For Sale" sign.

Then I fell off the gardening wagon with a vengeance. I'm enjoying creating my garden so much that yesterday when my men folk got together on the back deck for a cold one, I actually finished preparing my yellow bean bed before I joined them!

Let me explain about the three men who live with me, lest you think how lucky I am to have lots of help in the garden. There's my eighty-five-year-old father who helped me out once in my gardening business years ago, and sold gladiolus as onions. His contribution to my current gardening passion consists of wry remarks about all the dandelion wine I could be making, and reminiscing about the time I

planted twenty pounds of seed potatoes and harvested ten. When I write about the other two, my lodgers, I have to change their names to protect the guilty, so that should tell you something. "Nicholas," a theatre person, would rather have his nails pulled than get them dirty. He thinks the construction workers next door that I'm trying to hide are much more attractive than any garden could be. "Jake," an ex-tractor-trailer driver turned student, is like the snow-in-summer he buried when he decided to help me build the mound behind the tub; useful if you can control it.

Jake tries to take over the fun stuff that I want to do myself. Like my bathtub-trough-trickling-water project. Just because I let him mix the mortar, he thought he should get to position the rocks. I love playing with rocks. Then he informed me about his plan for making a fountain in three tiers from the ends of forty-gallon drums. "Sure," I said, "and maybe we could put a little tin bride and groom at the top." My plan is to make a natural looking waterfall with stones already hollowed a little by water, and maybe some driftwood.

Controlling Jake notwithstanding, it's been a good garden week since the "For Sale" sign came down. I've almost finished the bathtub project; dug bags of peaty soil and old horse manure; lugged home some great rocks; put up lattice; started a two-bin compost; planted the kitchen garden, some annuals in the front, and four big patio pots; cleaned up a lot of old boards and junk from behind the garage, and decided that's the perfect spot for a greenhouse.

I wonder if there are support groups for compulsive gardeners?

Gardengate — The Cover-Up

LOOKING AROUND AT SOME OF MY POLES and structures, I'm thinking that an important step in becoming a gin-and-tonic gardener is to become a master at cover-up. If it doesn't look good, hide it. Sure, you could change it, but in some cases, that involves a lot of work and/or expense. And sometimes it's out of your control, like a construction yard next door or the ugly side of a city building adjoining your property.

It's hard to sit back, book and drink in hand, with an eyesore disturbing your serenity and making you feel guilty. This is where it pays to remember that a clinging vine is not necessarily a bad thing to be. There are wonderful vines, perennial and annual, other than the types that keep you supplied with wine. Ugly walls, foundations, poles, rough banks, sheds, even dead trees can be made beautiful, or at least not ugly, with the right clinging vine.

My Aunt Gladys grew roses and lots of fussy things in her garden in Gander, but the thing I remember most is the Virginia creeper that covered the shed in the back corner. In the fall, it turned the most magnificent shades of red. I don't remember what the shed was made of, but Virginia creeper will adhere better to rough textures than to smooth. I've also seen it completely transforming a chain link fence, and the raw side of a ravine.

Boston ivy is probably the best hardy vine for clinging to walls. The leaves are large and glossy, and also gorgeous in the fall. According to Roscoe Fillmore, head gardener decades ago at Grand Pre Memorial Park, Nova Scotia, and whose wonderful books on gardening I inherited from my mother, the ivy won't hurt wood, but you'll have to tear it off, and sand away its tendrils in order to repaint. Or just don't repaint, which sounds like a good plan to me.

Ugly things can provide the same support for flowering vines as expensive trellis. Why waste money and time removing old poles and fences (or anything unsightly) when you can cover it with something beautiful like honeysuckle. Honeysuckle will also perfume the air, attract butterflies and birds, and is available in a variety of vines. Hall's is about the most vigorous and has creamy flowers. Scarlet trumpet is harder to find, but is worth the search. Honeysuckles like sun and well-drained soil.

Another great twiner is bittersweet, maybe called that because your joy in how fast it grows can turn to grief if it starts taking over. I've never had that problem, either because of the wrong growing conditions, or maybe my neglect. It isn't fussy about soil conditions, but it is fussy about its sex life. If you don't have a male and a female plant, you won't get the gorgeous orange berries that split open to scarlet in the fall, and look wonderful dried.

Of course, no matter how co-operative a perennial vine is in covering stuff quickly, it's not going to do it in one season. Annuals can take up the slack, so plant them around the perennial. You'll have to provide both with something to climb on. You could do it the old-fashioned way with nails and string, but netting is pretty cheap and a lot faster.

Scarlet Runner beans and Heavenly Blue morning glory are annuals that never let me down. Sow the Scarlet Runner beans right in the garden, and they'll reach about ten feet pretty quickly once they take off, fill up with sweet red flowers, and then give you long snap beans. If you pick them young (up to five inches) they're delicious, but it's also fun to lazily watch them grow to astonishing lengths of a foot or more. Then you can dry the seeds and freeze them for next year, if you're so inclined.

You can't sow morning glory transplants as early as some annuals. Well you can, but they just won't do anything, because they like warmth. If seedlings aren't available at a local supplier, you can sow the seeds in June. I didn't get mine in one year until late June, after putting them in hot tap water and letting them sit overnight. They were late flowering but just watching them climb the railing where I sit with my morning coffee still pleased me no end. Some of the newer hybrids are more tolerant of the midday sun and will stay open longer, but I'm kind of partial to the old Heavenly Blue.

I can't close without a climbing nasturtium rave. Sow them right in the garden. They love poor soil, tolerate drought, climb or sprawl to six feet, bloom in six weeks, and have edible flowers, leaves, and seeds. God, I love nasturtiums.

JUNE

Sweet Seduction (I Hope)

I SPENT AN AFTERNOON POKING around rural nurseries in the southwest corner of Newfoundland this week. I've already done the local ones of course, but you never know what the growers outside of town might have potted up. The beauty of knowing who's got what in containers is that anytime you have a little mad money, you can add something permanent to your garden. I found two good smallish nurseries that I didn't know existed, both with prices well below their town competitors, and one specializing in growing native trees from seed. Wherever you live, it's always worth your while (and fun) to check out as many plant sources as possible.

I would have been happy to come home from my excursion with one Virginia creeper but I found some that were so big, and so reasonably priced, I bought two. One I've planted on the street corner of my lot, to grow both ways on the bluish-grey picket fence. The other I'll plant by the ten-foot fence section between me and the heavy equipment next door. I also came home with two robust rugosa roses that have gone in along the driveway with two similar clumps that were a gift from a neighbour. I spaced them about four feet apart. If I get ambitious in the fall, I'll take up the grass between each one to encourage them to fill in the whole space quicker. Two climbing roses full of buds, Don Juan and Golden Showers, took the last of the forty dollars of cash I had on me. I'm not familiar with Don Juan (in the horticultural sense), but he's already lived up to his name by seducing me out of ten dollars with his bronze-coloured leaves and virile look.

The yellow Golden Showers is at the driveway corner of the house, in theory to be trained around both walls. Near the driveway end of the front fence, one of the fence posts is about three feet longer than the others for some reason. I kept meaning to saw it off, until I realized it's the perfect perch for my old cedar bird feeder. Now as I sit at my computer I can watch the birds, and, soon, I hope, enjoy the red Don Juan clambering over the fence and up the post, a thorny but beautiful barrier between birds and Bushka, the cat.

It amazes me that forty dollars could buy me six such large, healthy specimens, when the same amount wouldn't have bought a dozen small perennials in town. I want so many of those that I've decided the only way to go is to grow them myself.

Out behind my garage was an old wooden box-like thing, about two feet by five feet, with eight-inch sides. I have no idea what it was, but it's survived two or three cleanups because I just knew it would come in handy for something. Ditto with four old scrap lumber sawhorse thingys. With the help of a few old planks, I now have a work bench outside the back garage door. Nails in the wall above it keep my hand tools semi-organized, and fifty-cents worth of huge hooks at a yard sale hold the hoses waiting to be fixed.

On the other side of the door I now have a perennial planting table. I'll put some plastic in the box, with drainage holes, and then a good layer of beach rocks before I put in the soil. I'll be able to start, and tend, hundreds of perennials without bending over, until I set them out in September! And won't I be proud of myself next year!

Everything seems to be muddling along okay except for my Scarlet Runner beans. Not a sign of them yet, and they went in days before the yellow bush beans, which are well up. The yellow ones are in full sun and good garden soil. The Scarlet Runners are in peaty stuff, half-day sun, and sit under the garage overhang where they don't get as much natural water. I'll give them another few days, but I have a feeling I'm not going to get away with using that peaty soil as is. Oh well, any gin-and-tonic gardener worth her salt would have tried to.

High Heels?

MY SCARLET RUNNERS ARE FINALLY UP, so maybe by August I'll have flowers and by September even beans. It's coming back to me now that my garden was usually a few weeks behind those of really serious gardeners even when I was a bit serious myself. That's partly because I'm always late planting, and because I spend more time thinking about feeding and watering than actually doing it. Deep in my heart I feel that if I go to all the trouble of preparing the soil and planting the seeds, it's not unreasonable to expect Mother Nature to do the rest. I know of course that this isn't logical unless you plant only things that Nature would have put there herself, and if I waited a hundred years, she never would have put runner beans on the side of my garage. The thing is, I have to be reasonable and logical in so many aspects of life, I just refuse to have that pressure on me in the garden.

Actually, I've gone out twice to buy fertilizer, and couldn't make up my mind what to buy. (Indecision when it comes to spending money isn't really cured by "the plan"). I did buy bone meal and food for the roses, but I haven't gotten around to feeding anything else. Now when I walk around the garden, I feel like the other stuff is silently accusing me of loving the roses best, which I guess I do, but it's not nice to show it.

On this morning's walk around the garden I discovered that slugs have been visiting. Now I really feel guilty, because of course they don't bother roses, so it didn't even occur to me to buy slug bait. I do, however, have an ample supply of wood ashes saved from my stove last winter, which makes wonderful slug deterrent. It just doesn't work real well unless you actually take it out of the garage and spread a little border around your beds. Then the slugs can't crawl through it.

This is obviously one of my days of remorse for being a very relaxed gardener, so I might as well confess the lot. I completely screwed up my compost pile by being too lackadaisical to chop up the sods before I put them in. If you just bury them upside down in a bed, they will eventually decompose, but in the compost pile, full sods make it impossible to turn! So I have this great mound of clippings and peelings, eggshells and coffee scraps, fresh manure and sods—too many sods—that I can barely get a fork into, let alone turn. I think maybe I'll just cover it with topsoil and use it as a zucchini and cucumber hill, and start another compost pile. There's always a way around making too much work for yourself!

On the bright side, I've started laying a natural stone patio in the soil out back between the bathtub and the deck. (Now that it's all covered in mortar and rocks, and actually ready for fish or lilies or whatever, I still can't stop calling it the bathtub.) I love picking stone so much that if I'm not careful I could become a menace on the highway. I'll be driving along, and spot a nice flat, colourful one down in the ditch, and slam on the brakes. That's bad enough, but the fact that I actually spot these rocks while I'm driving is a little scary too.

I lay them all out, flattest side up, and then I have the most fun piecing the patio together. It's kind of like doing a jigsaw puzzle only better because you're the designer. Jake observed that the surface was a little rough. "Women in high heels will be tripping on those stones," he said. This is his first summer with me, or else he'd know why I found that so funny. Nobody would wear high heels to the type of summer entertaining that I do. Anyway, by the time I'm finished it will be level enough to suit my needs, even if I have to be a bit careful where I lay down a glass. But maybe I should keep some spare sandals on hand, just in case I ever do have a summer visitor wearing high heels.

What Every Garden Needs

YOU KNOW GARDENS AND HAMMOCKS go together like, well, gin and tonic. I don't have any trees big enough yet for hanging a hammock, so when I heard of a freestanding one at a nearby yard sale, I had to go take a look. It was all wrapped up, white metal tubes, and blue striped hammock. It matched the colour of my house, and the seller showed me one in the catalogue just like it for five times the price, so now it's out back on the grass, angled so I can't see the still-unfinished stone patio. (It's almost finished. Of course, breaking in the hammock may delay things a bit, but it is inspirational.) Yesterday, after spending two hours figuring out how to put the thing together, I took my book and tried it out. I discovered right away the big advantages of a freestanding hammock: you can follow the sun, change your view, take it to the beach....

With the mid-afternoon sun behind my head so that it's not in my eyes while I read, I'm facing the slope up to the weathered picket fence. Because the land drops away down to the road on the other side, what I see when I'm lying there is the expanse of fence outlined against the sky. It's a wonderful canvas that can be seen only by some-one lying down in my hammock, and now my mind is racing with the prospect of what to plant there. It almost feels like a secret, and I'm really excited about it.

I love the grey softness of the unpainted fence. I won't offend it with anything bright or bold, or cover too much of it. I think one white rambling rose, and lavender or periwinkle stuff. Periwinkle! There I was trying to think of things with periwinkle-coloured flow-ers, forgetting all about the colour's namesake. Some of that along the base, and creeping up, definitely.

The rose I want would be a repeat flowerer, single blooms, fragrant, leaves not too dark, and nice fall hips for the birds. So the search is on. *The New Rose Expert* by Dr. D.G. Hessayon has yielded noth-ing that fits all the above criteria. Kiftsgate is a midsum-mer bloomer, but the bright red hips sound good. Likewise for Rambling Rector. Wedding Day looks wonderful, but it doesn't mention hips. And a problem with that book is that it's British.

I really need to get a North American one. My old *Green Thumbs* by Roscoe Fillmore mentions Seven Sisters, sometimes called Thousand Beauties, with flowers fading from rose to white, giving a multi-coloured effect. That sounds glorious, but I don't think I want any pinks in this particular palette. Also, that book is so old, I don't know if I could even find Seven Sisters. I've never seen it anywhere.

There's a telephone pole in my canvas that I want to hide. It's actually across the street, or I'd be trying to grow something over it. It's off to one side, and I'm thinking a small flowering crab species, maybe a weeping one, might frame that side nicely. Or it might be too much. We'll see.

Speaking of climbing roses, the buds on the yellow one I planted on the side of the house are opening and they're red. That rose was definitely tagged yellow, but I don't really mind. I have a yellow one on the corner, even though it finished blooming last week. Maybe I'll get another flush out of it in the fall. I've got lots more places for climbers anyway.

My cosmos are behaving very strangely. The ones in the container are bushing out and blooming beautifully; the ones in the ground keep drying out. It should be the other way around. The soil in the garden looks fine, but the cosmos are definitely not happy there.

I think sometimes a garden just wants to let you know who's boss.

Tough Love

I JUST CUT DOWN A TREE. It was only a little tree, five minutes work with my little bucksaw. I mention it here for two reasons: knowing when to cut down a tree can save you a lot of grief and guilt down the road, and I'm feeling very nostalgic about my little bucksaw.

But first things first: of course I like trees. I'd actually like to have a few more trees, so why did I want to cut one down? Mainly because it was in the wrong place. It blocked the view from my office when I lifted my eyes from my computer. It also wasn't particularly nice, and I have three others like it, so it really wasn't worth the trouble of moving it; and besides, eventually it would have shaded Don Juan too much. If I had let it go another few years, it would have been harder for me to cut down physically, and a little harder emotionally too.

I'm such a sook I don't even like thinning things, but I am determined to be the one in control in this garden. I've seen people let volunteer trees completely take over their gardens. Not me. No more Mr. Nice Guy!

After all, I am the woman who agreeably divided up the crystal and the silver, but made sure I got custody of the bucksaw. It's a sweet little thing with a red handle, and I bought it years ago. It comes in handy for all sorts of things, not just in the garden, is much easier to use than a handsaw, and much more useful to a "re-single" woman than the Wedgwood service for twelve.

Anyway the tree is gone and I bet nobody will miss it. It was one of the six planted like soldiers along the front of the property by the previous owner. One of the remaining five is a fir about four feet high. It's nice and full, with a good shape. I don't like where it is either, but it's definitely worth saving, so I'll either work around it or move it. If I move it early in the fall, it should have time to get well established before the winter sets in. I translate early fall to late August in our climate, just to be on the safe side. Trees can also be moved in the early spring, before they break dormancy, but again, you might as well be realistic about your climate. Our springs are so erratic, with freeze/thaw/freeze/thaw that I think trees have enough to cope with, without being moved around. And I have enough to cope with, without trying to move a tree before it wakes up, because if the weather hasn't been warm enough to stir a tree, it sure isn't going to stir me.

What will stir me in the spring will be to have lots and lots of little perennials and biennials to play with; which means I should start them now from seed, because I could never afford to buy all that I want. I want masses of two types: old-fashioned types, like hollyhocks and delphiniums and foxgloves; and wildflower types, like black-eyed Susan, butterfly weed, and shasta daisies. I also need lots of creeping thyme for between the patio stones. Earlier in the season there were seeds for all this and more, everywhere I looked. I didn't buy any then, of course, and now I'm having trouble finding them. I did come across plants of a most wonderful, flat variety of lemon thyme. Not only does it smell heavenly, but it has both bright green and deep yellow leaves (not variegated, but two totally different coloured leaves on the same plant). It would elevate my patio to the divine. Now I have to find out if this type will take walking on, and where I can get seeds for it. Just once, I'd like to be able to buy what I like for the garden and not worry about money!

JULY

Marigold, Witch Hazel, and Alder Branches—A Matter of Taste

HOT SUNNY DAYS ARE THE KISS OF DEATH, or life, depending on how you look at it, for gin-and-tonic gardeners. This is when we are at our most vulnerable, exposed, if you will, especially if you live next door to a really serious gardener. I think of a gardener I know who I shall call "Marigold." She's nice enough, but really earnest and, dare I say it, a bit too stiff for my taste. She probably thinks of me as Witch Hazel, marginally useful in the garden, not very fussy, and more suited to wild or natural settings.

The problem is one of priorities. When Marigold wakes in the morning to a hot-day forecast, she gets her gardening done right away. I plan, or even make, supper, because I certainly don't want to have to do that on a sunny afternoon, and we do have to eat.

Sometimes by the time I get around to gardening, it's too hot, and I console myself with the thought that you really shouldn't water during hot sun, so I put it all off until the evening. Then my deck seems to attract people, and I don't work well when others are sitting around relaxing. If this good weather holds, I'm going to have to be like the three little pigs and keep getting up earlier every morning so that I can relax with a clear conscience.

I remember one sunny summer when it rained almost every night. That was perfect. I even mulched early that year, and managed to almost wear out a hammock. Watering is key, even more so than feeding, and most of us water too little or too frequently. A soaking for a few hours once a week is infinitely better than a daily sprinkling. My dream garden has a watering system that simply requires turning the taps on and off; no standing there holding the hose, no dragging it around, or moving sprinklers from one spot to another. This dream is possible, but requires a bit of planning and a few dollars. If you're prepared to invest both, most gardening books, or local landscape companies can help you out. You can even get a system with a timer so you don't even have to turn the taps. Now that's my idea of watering. As soon as I decide if I'm going to stay in this house for the foreseeable future, I'm going to investigate an add-on underground soaker system. I can spend hours sitting in the sun designing that, and not feel a bit guilty!

Next to an automatic watering system, mulch is right up there as a gin-and-tonic gardener's best friend. Not only does it keep moisture in the soil longer, it discourages weeds. The question is not whether to mulch, but with what. My answer to that is with whatever is available. I've used grass clippings, seaweed, evergreen needles and sprigs, leaves, and sawdust. Commercial mulches like shredded bark, chips, and nuggets are attractive, but have the disadvantage of costing money. I'd rather use up something nature provides and save my money for plants or refreshments. Besides, garden beauty is like any other; it's in the eye of the beholder. I visited a gardening friend this week, looking for inspiration. His tidy garden is full of straight rows of wee veggies, and I know I'll envy him his harvest but you know what impressed me the most? The lovely alder branches he was inserting to stake his early peas. He actually apologized for them. They were cut uniformly enough to satisfy a neat freak, but still had a natural appeal impossible with conventional stakes. I've been somewhat intimidated by his industriousness, and meticulously groomed garden, but the alder stakes reassured me. Of course you have to be industrious to cut stakes instead of buying them, but at least I now feel we have something in common. His alder branches looked so nice I almost rushed out and bought some more seeds. Almost. I really should finish a few other projects first. Soon. Some early morning or late evening, or the next not-so-fine day.

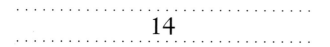

Musings of Monkshood, Mallow, and Men

THE STARS OF MY GARDEN SO FAR this summer have been white perennial mallow and monkshood, neither of which I planted. However I do take the credit for how good they now look. It was obvious they were there when I moved in, of course, but they were just a tangled mess. The mallow in particular looked weak and scraggly. I wasn't particularly fond of it; insipid stuff, I thought.

Now I love it. I cannot believe how bright and reliable it has been all summer. I think I may have put a little bit of fertilizer around, but all it really took to make these two old timers happy was severe weeding at the beginning of the summer. Now if only I could give them space to spread. They're together in the narrow strip along the front of the house. And I mean narrow; about a foot of earth held in by a concrete walkway. If it weren't for that darn walkway, I'd probably have great stands of the stuff like I see in other gardens around town.

I've considered taking up the walkway, but it would probably be easier to dig a bed on the other side of it, divide the clumps, and transplant the babies.

The mallow is intriguing me. It's a very common old-fashioned perennial in Newfoundland gardens and I've never paid much attention to it. Now that I've decided I like it, I've been trying to look it up in my books, and I'm not finding much! It shows up on English abbey gardening lists in the twelfth century, and quite possibly the seed was brought here with the early settlers. Maybe it's so common that it gets totally overlooked, or maybe, just maybe, I'm calling it the wrong name and it isn't mallow at all. The flower is similar to but smaller than the annual mallow, lavatera, and I think I've heard it called musk. The only reference I could find to musk mallow describes the flower as red-violet. Our Newfoundland varieties are pale pink and white. I have just a few pink ones volunteering by the back bridge. I'll save some seed this year, and try to increase those; anything that persistent is my kind of plant!

Monkshood is another reliable old-fashioned perennial that isn't particularly stylish anymore. I inherited two types with this house: a solid dark purple, and a softer purple shading to white, which is a late bloomer. Monkshood was also common in the Middle Ages, perhaps hence its name. It's often described as being shade loving and blooming late summer. Mine is in full sun and has been blooming since early July, so go figure. I don't know why it's not more popular; it's a very stalwart plant. Maybe the name is a little stern, but the plant itself seems to be pretty easy going.

In trying to read up on monkshood and mallow, I got into one of my gardening books that I haven't read for a while: *English Cottage Gardens* by Edward Hyams. A few chapters of that and I'm yearning for a thatched roof. I always have a highlighter handy when I'm reading, and I notice one of the things I highlighted in this book is, "the women never worked in the vegetable gardens. That was man's work."

Some of these old sexist concepts weren't so bad. I've personally never found a man who liked to garden, and the concept of relying on one for my vegetables is amusingly foreign to me. It's an interesting fantasy, though. I might be totally smitten if I met a man who asked me for a walk on the beach and brought a garbage bag for seaweed, who didn't think Vigoro was the latest sex drug, and who knew that a six-pack isn't necessarily something you drink or something you envy in a younger man's stomach. And if he could make a thatched roof, and cook those vegetables....

Sometimes a little fantasy goes a long way!

Give Me a Wild Rose Any Day

I MIGHT HAVE KNOWN A ROSE NAMED DON JUAN would give me trouble! I bought him from the same nursery, in the same prime condition, and planted him at the same time, as Golden Showers (both climbers). Golden Showers has already bloomed and is in bud again. Don Juan not only hasn't bloomed, but is decidedly unwell.

He had one lovely bud and glossy dark green leaves when I fell for him. The bud didn't open, and I found the whole stem on the ground one day looking almost chewed off. That may be canker, or maybe it got broken by the lawn mower, although I can't imagine how. Now he has aphids, and is in the early stages of mildew, and—this could happen only to me—I think he's going blind!

Yes, blind! According to my rose book, an empty wheat-like husk instead of a flower bud on top of a mature stem is called blindness. Causes, it says, are many and varied; may be frost damage (no), lack of food (I don't think so), shortage of light (nah). What about bird droppings, I wonder? Some of those in the eye would do it for me, and I did have the brainwave to plant Don Juan under the bird feeder so he could climb up the post. I know I said if it has to be fussed with, I don't want it in my garden (so why is she growing roses, you might ask) but I can't stand to see him suffer like that. So I'll move him, trim him, feed him, spray him, in short, give him some symbolic cane to grow on, and if he doesn't appreciate my efforts and shape up, get rid of him! Maybe I wouldn't be so harsh if his name was Dona Juanita, but the very last thing I need is another fussy male to look after.

I confess I'm not even going to rush out and do this today because Daughter #2 is coming to visit and needs a beach fix. So, the only roses I'm going to be communing with today are the wild ones surrounding my fishing shack.

The stones are all laid for the patio. They're a little rough, but they look good. The biggest nuisance now will be keeping the weeds out of the cracks until I have the creeping thyme ready for transplanting. Considering that I haven't even planted the seed yet, that may not be until next spring, or maybe October if I'm lucky. Any practical person would have planted the thyme before she started the rocks, but what's that got to do with me?

I finally found the seeds. I've built the seed box, and now I'm waiting on the soil. I searched the garage and found some pieces of pink insulation that I'm going to encase in plastic and use to line the bottom of the box. The plastic is important because if the fibreglass insulation gets wet, it's of no use. Styrofoam would be better, but that's not what I had lying around. The purpose of it is to provide bottom protection through the winter. Because the seed box is built on a waist-high stand, just covering the top won't protect seedlings I might want to overwinter. The insulation might not do the trick either, so I'll just leave a few there this winter to test it out. I could also move the whole box to the ground, but that won't do the old wood any good. It also wouldn't thaw and warm up nearly as early in the spring, or be as accessible for conversion to a cold frame, which I plan to do with old windows if I can find any that fit. Otherwise, I'll just make a top with some plastic and scraps.

Enough of that. Down by my shack, wild roses and beach peas are blooming. Sea grass is waving and raspberries are ripening. That's really my kind of garden.

Puttering and Patience

CONTRARY TO ANY IMPRESSION I MAY HAVE GIVEN, my favourite garden activity actually isn't lying in the hammock, sipping a cold drink and reading. The thing I love the very best, or at least as much, about gardening (and housekeeping) is puttering. And I take strong exception to the *Encyclopedia Britannia*'s definition: "to work in a dawdling or ineffective manner…to waste time." Puttering in the garden is not only effective, it's the most effective way to look after a garden without killing yourself with work or burdening yourself with guilt.

Spending even a few minutes each day puttering around, pulling up the scattered weeds, snipping off faded blooms, tying up something lanky, makes all the difference. I've come to the harsh realization that I haven't been very good at puttering in the garden this summer. I talk about it well, and I do think about it often, but I don't get down to actually doing it nearly as regularly as I should.

I blame some of that on circumstance; lots of visitors around this summer, and I'm no good at working, even puttering, when there are people about. But another part of it is impatience. A garden that is lush and a little overgrown, and looks like it's been there for years awakens the putterer in me. It's going to take some time before mine comes anywhere near that, and suddenly I have this longing for instant gratification. There's a house for sale down the street with a large old garden full of wonderful stuff: a massive Blanc Double de Coubert rose hedge, two enormous Bridal Wreath spireas, spires of deep wine and pale pink hollyhocks, clumps of mallow and monkshood. I went for a look. It's a great house. I'd have no end of fun puttering there. Then I strolled home and looked at my relatively bare plot, and accepted that all I can do (short of moving) is to get a few largish shrubs, some great clumps of things, and a fast-growing tree or two, planted before next season. With two daughters heading back to university, I don't have much (understatement) of a budget for this, but nurseries often have sales at this time of year, or later in the fall, on containerized stock that can be planted at anytime.

The best way to get big clumps of perennials is to dig your own from a friend's garden, and some shrubs and trees you can get from the wild. This is trickier, but can certainly be done successfully, especially if you wait until the tree has gone into dormancy in the fall. I have a cherry tree lined up from a friend, neither sweet nor really sour (the cherries, not the friend), perfect for preserving in a sugar syrup and black rum (or brandy or whatever). I'm also going to start looking in the woods for a nice mountain ash. They're common in Eastern Canada, and given space, won't grow too big for most gardens. In the spring, they have nice white flowers in flat clusters, but the bright red berries in the fall are the highlight of this tree. The birds love them, and I've read that if you invert them in a jar of brine, they will keep for Christmas decorating. With good freebies, and a Charles Joly lilac that Baby Sister bought me when she was visiting, I may be able to justify springing for a decent size flowering crab.

I just have to be patient, as all gardeners do. Sometimes you really should wait for a garden to show you what to do. For instance, I've finished mounding soil and stuff around the tub, and now the mound is ready to be planted. With only a curve of stepping stones for the fairies, and the one clump of day lilies, and three of snow-in-summer that I stuck in there earlier, it has an attractive Japanese look. I had planned it to be full of flowering clumps and hummocks of things, but now a bonsai-looking larch, leaning and twisted, keeps coming into my mind's eye. Kept to the back corner, it would give strong balance to the whole composition.

I don't mind the garden telling me what to do; as long as we don't forget who's boss.

AUGUST

A Little Parenting Lesson

SUDDENLY IT'S THE BEGINNING OF AUGUST, I have company coming, and I even haven't finished the patio/tub project. And my little back bridge (deck) is even smaller now because I cut part of it off to make the patio, and I haven't actually finished my waist-high perennial seed bed for all the seeds I haven't found yet!

Why don't I ever learn to finish one thing before I start another? I'm in the very spot I swore I would never be in again; can't relax in the garden because everywhere I look I see work undone. I have to put a push on this week, and at least get all the stones laid so Baby Sister and I can lie around without tripping over a pile every time we get up to rub lotion on each other.

I also have to be as attentive to the drinking and eating habits of my containers as I am to my own if I want to maintain any shred of my dignity as a gardener. Either that, or fill everything with nasturtiums next year because they don't like to be fed, or even watered, too much.

My containers are all fairly large, and don't dry out quickly, but even so, the only thing for a person like me to do is to set a regular time for watering, and get into the habit, sort of like exercising. (I'm not so good at that, either, come to think of it.) The evening is best, so the water can really sink in and get absorbed before the sun can dry it up. Some plants are sensitive to damp foliage at night, but I've never had any trouble with my container plants. I try not to get the foliage wet, but I don't really worry about it.

And while I'm on the subject of watering, Nicholas and I gathered an enormous bunch of wildflowers this week, in honour of his visiting friend, and put them in about a quart of water in a stone crock. The next day, they were very droopy, and I discovered they had soaked up every bit of the water! I don't know if wildflowers are thirstier than cultivated ones, but if you're going to tramp around ditches picking flowers, you want them to last longer than a day, so check the water often.

I've found purple coneflower Starlight and blanket flower for my own wildflower garden, and I've also found the seeds for some thyme to plant between the patio stones. It's called wild thyme (*Thymus serpyllum*). The pack says, "trails and spreads over your garden like a thick luxurious pile carpet. Ideal for between paving. Dense tiny leaves smother weeds and have a pleasant

scent. Shades of white and rose to near purple." Now doesn't that sound too good to be true? I bought two packs at $4.99 each, expensive seeds and twice as many as I need, just in case it's only half as good as it sounds and doesn't germinate profusely. It's that kind of logic and optimism that sustains me as a gardener.

Sometimes of course, stronger sustenance is called for, hence the name of this book. Like the weekend when another friend of Nicholas visited. Instead of being impressed with my accomplishments, he almost accused me of lying to my readers because my garden didn't live up to his expectations.

This man obviously knows nothing about gardening. I bet his wife does all of theirs. What I have here is a labour of love in progress. The creation of a new garden has to be savoured and contemplated. You don't decide one day you'd like to have a child, and the next day have one, full grown.

You want to maximize the pleasure of the conception, minimize the labour pains along the way, guide and enjoy every stage of its growth. But you also have to know how to relax and enjoy life, because a fussy smothering parent does not end up with a strong independent child...garden.

That's my philosophizing for the week.

Just Tie the Pantyhose to the Wagon

BEING BOTH A CONFIRMED DO-IT-YOURSELFER, and a starving writer, it was somewhat unusual this summer for me to have ordered a half-pickup load of what my local nurseryman calls mineral soil. My normal routine for a bit of soil would be to find a good spot in the countryside and dig a few bags; one of the perks of Newfoundland living. I've found in the past that what many landscaping companies deliver for topsoil doesn't seem to have much humus content.

For twenty dollars, I got enough lovely, screened stuff to fill my seed box, and mound over all the rubble surrounding the tub/pool. To get enough bagged potting soil just to fill the seed box (two feet by five feet by six inches) would have cost close to twenty dollars or more. Perennial seeds are expensive, and some are very tiny, so it was better not to use garden soil for the seed box. The creeping thyme, for example, needs light to germinate, so you just sprinkle it on top of the soil and gently firm it. The rougher the soil, the harder tiny seeds, or any seeds, have to struggle to get started. But I'm only now realizing the biggest bonus of all—no weed seeds in this soil at all.

I was a bit worried about the prospect of keeping the mound weed-free until I could get it all planted and established, but so far, not a weed in sight. So, it pays to ask a local nursery about soil.

Of course it pays to do a lot of things in the garden that I don't do, which, I suppose, is why I'm so tickled when I do something efficient, like a serious gardener. Efficient things like using bits of cut up old pantyhose to tie things up with, because the nylon is very strong, but won't damage the plants. I heard this tip years ago, but the other day didn't I use string anyway to tie a cane of climbing Don Juan to the fence simply because I just didn't happen to have a piece of

pantyhose handy. That's what I get for wearing pants all the time. Of course the string sliced Don Juan's longest cane in two. I know I'm fed up with Don Juan anyway, but a real gardener who knew about pantyhose strips would whip out the scissors when she got a run, and have a supply on hand all the time. Knee-highs will work just as well, and that will be one of my New Year's resolutions.

I'm tickled with some of my recent yard sale purchases too, the best one being a little red wagon. What a useful thing in the garden, for weeding, lugging stuff when the wheelbarrow is in use, or following the sun with potted plants. I also got a great galvanized pail with a handle, thinking I'd use it as a planter, but maybe I'll save it for filling with ice, and bottles of wine and beer, or sand and candles, at intimate patio gatherings; which I will have, next year. (Another resolution).

And here's the last one for today. I need to walk more, but I find just walking sort of boring. I'm going to start walking on streets where there are interesting gardens, and whenever I see the gardeners, stop and talk, and shamelessly ask for seeds, or bits of stuff. Most gardeners love exchanging tips and experience and whatever they have an excess of, and this is the time for gathering.

A possible answer to my earlier musing of why monkshood isn't more popular; I've been informed the plant is poisonous if ingested. I've never heard that before, but that would certainly make anyone with small children avoid it. It also makes me wonder what other garden plants are poisonous, especially with edible flowers being so popular these days. I served nasturtiums in a salad the other day, and felt very chic (even though nobody ate them.)

A New Best Friend?

WHEN I LIE IN THE HAMMOCK READING, I'm facing the mound and the tub, so I'm really doing two things at once; reading, and waiting for inspiration about what else to plant there.

Choosing the plant material shouldn't be difficult. It finally came to me that the reason I'm hesitating about it is because I don't really feel the bones are finished. It needs some-thing tall, something else architectural. Having decided that, I realize that it may take me a while to find the right piece. I picked up a curlicued headboard and f   o   o   t   b   o   a   r   d of an iron bed for ten dollars at a yard sale, and fooled around with that on, behind, and around, the mound for a while, but it didn't work. They'll come in handy sometime though, maybe at right

angles cornering a bed of something.

Another thing that might work is a weeping standard (a growing form achieved with grafting, could be roses, could be something else) about the size of a Siberian pea shrub, except I don't particularly like them. In fact, I'm not particularly fond of standards period. They always look somewhat contrived to me, as they are of course, with the foliage and flower part grafted on top of a long skinny trunk. But I do love weeping things in gardens, and I like the thought of delicately swaying branches and trickling water together. A dwarf (very dwarf) weeping willow would be lovely, but I don't even know if such a thing exists. I'm going to order every catalogue I can get my hands on this fall, because there's probably just the thing out there somewhere, and I can spend all winter looking for it.

My walking and garden visiting routine has already paid off. I've been admiring some very large clusters of flattish, reddish flowers, and wondering what they were. I finally spied the gardener, and was surprised when she told me they were clumps of bee balm. I've never grown bee balm because I thought I didn't like it. The individual flowers that you see on the seed packets look kind of scruffy, but en masse, and at a little distance, it's a very attractive plant. And it spreads rapidly. That could be a problem in limited space, but with all the grass I'm dying to get rid off, bee balm sounds like it could be my new best friend.

There are a few varieties, in shades of red and white, and they bloom from June through August. The ones I saw were around four feet high, in clumps just about as wide. From a few department-store plants three years ago, this lucky gardener has gotten all this beauty, supplied her neighbour with the same, and—big bonus—attracted a hummingbird. No small feat, since hummingbirds are uncommon in Newfoundland. She had her bee balm in a border, but my *Crockett's Flower Garden* includes bee balm with perennials that are large and dramatic enough to be planted in their own site and allowed to naturalize. Other perennials that James Underwood Crockett puts into this category are peonies, New England asters, day lilies, and irises. I think I'd add oriental poppies, shasta daisies, and phlox to that list.

I'm really getting a jump-start on the garden next year. Tiny creeping thyme, blanket flower, purple coneflower, Iceland poppies, Pacific Giant delphiniums, Excelsior Mix foxgloves, Canterbury Bells, Nora Barlow columbine, and giant single mixed hollyhocks are peeking through the soil in my seed box. I picked up another lilac, a nice big full one called Sensation that the nursery woman tells me has a white-edged flower. And I now know where to get bee balm.

It's been raining too much lately for much walking and garden visiting, but there's still lots of time to divide and transplant any perennials I may be offered.

There's still lots of time for roses to bloom, thank goodness. I almost pulled up the one straggly specimen that came with the house this spring; it looked so dead. But I left it, and totally forgot about it. The other day I discovered it has two canes, and two buds, one more than it had last year; this in spite of being totally neglected, and over-grown by yellow loosestrife. I feel as though a wastrel has returned, even though we all know who the real wastrel is in this garden. And this tough cookie is exactly the kind of plant a gin-and-tonic gar-dener needs!

I am very contrite, and will make it up to it next year.

Gardener, Know Thyself

GARDENING (OR LANDSCAPING), can be divided into two distinct categories: softscaping and hardscaping. The softscaping is the planting and growing of the greenery that we traditionally think of as gardening. Hardscaping covers stone and wooden structures, walls, walkways, and statuary.

They're equally important. Japanese gardens rely more heavily on the elements of earth, stone, and water than on plants; many North American gardeners rely solely on plants and ignore the hardscaping elements. I really like them. What I need is a partner to garden with, one who is as into growing as I am into wood and stone and structural elements. I had this epiphany this weekend, when I spent an afternoon at my beach cottage.

There had been quite a wind; the beach was full of dried seaweed, fresh kelp, and driftwood. I could have brought home bags of enrichment for my soil. I had also planned to search out and mark some wild specimens to transplant in the spring. I wanted to do those things, but

I was seduced by the driftwood. I spent the entire afternoon walking on the beach, lugging back curved grey spirits of the land and sea, first picturing them embraced by living things not yet planted, then expanding to gardens not yet seen.

There was so much of it, and no beachcombers but me. And I kept gathering: A helmeted soldier's bust, flat on the bottom from a saw, neck and head carved by a beaver; a sea serpent, standing large, with piercing eyes; whale's tails, poised in crotch wood.

And so I came home with the car full of driftwood. No seaweed, no transplants branded. Not even the bouquet of vermilion wild rose hips that I've been looking forward to all summer.

With driftwood you can't afford to wait. Next week's seas might change the pickings totally. And for me, that sea serpent, easily six feet long and three feet high, more than makes up for the fact that my small perennials in the seed box aren't looking so good because I forgot to water them in my haste to get to the beach. I'm sure they'll recover, but I can buy the plants next spring if I have to; my serpent is a one-of a-kind treasure. There are so many "cute" things you can buy, adapt, or create for garden sculpture. A lot of them are too cute for my taste. I think you can't go wrong if you stick to natural elements: stone, wood, or even brick. I'm sure there are times when bright paint is better than natural tones, but not

for me. Weathered wood and mossy stones lend much more garden character than polyethylene and concrete, although even concrete can be softened by aggregate and colouring. Applying buttermilk or plain yoghurt, mixed with a little live moss, will quickly give concrete an aged appearance. And fresh paint can look centuries old, or not like paint at all, with little effort or skill.

Some of the most interesting gardens I've seen contain pieces of architectural salvage: mantles, columns, doors, almost anything with shape and texture. Whenever I go to a yard sale or junk store now, my eye is seeing what things might be instead of what they are.

The sunburst trim from around a broken wall clock echoes the sunflowers against the garage wall. A clay chimney flue cascades with lobelia. A potbelly stove accents a bed or overflows with ivy.

But beauty in the garden, like anywhere else, is very much in the eye of the beholder. If your taste runs to flamingos and gnomes, you should have them. But think about opening up your imagination to non-traditional use of all kinds of stuff. If you do need to paint something in the garden, either follow Nature's palette or go wild and really have some fun with it. The garden can absorb all kinds of creations that the house would reject.

Winter, of course, is the perfect time for working on garden art, sculpture, furniture, or whatever. My "interesting-junk-for-long-winter-days" collection in the garage is growing. It now includes three rusty anchors in different sizes.

Haven't quite decided what to do with them yet.

SEPTEMBER

To Bulb or Not to Bulb

BY THE TIME I'M PSYCHOLOGICALLY READY for spring bulbs (around March), it's months too late. All those tulips and daffodils that you see when the snow finally departs have been in the ground all winter, just waiting to remind us of the cycle of life and spring, of hope eternal, and all that stuff. It's as clear as life itself; you plant spring bulbs in the fall. The bulbs you plant in the spring are called summer bulbs, and there's actually a crocus that blooms in the fall that you can plant in the summer.

Thinking back to my experience with spring bulbs in Former Life (F.L.), Newfoundland, I won't be planting tulips out in the garden for a few years yet. The problem is the foliage after the blooms are finished. It's not pretty, but if you cut if off, you ruin the flower for the next year. Bulbs draw the strength they need to rejuvenate, and start the growth cycle all over again, from the foliage as it dies back. With our late spring, the only way I've figured out to avoid having to look at dying tulip leaves well into the summer is to plant tulips in amongst large clumps of fast-growing perennials, and I don't have many of those yet.

In F.L., I sometimes used to dig them all up after they'd finished blooming (hundreds of them), heel them in (lay them in a shallow trench and cover up the bulbs) out back, dry them off when the leaves turned brown, store them, and then plant them again in the fall.

That was around the time I realized I needed a new life! In this lifetime, I think pots would be my answer for tulips. Tulips, like all bulbs, look better planted in clumps. So I'd fill a few pots, sink them right into the ground, take them up when they're finished blooming, plant annuals in that space, and stick the pots down again in the fall. Oh yeah, there's more than one way to get around a tulip, for they can be glorious. You could do up big pots for the patio. Any nursery will tell you how to winterize these in your area, and also how to force some pots for spring blooms inside. Of course if you're in a warm climate, forcing them is about your only hope. It's not hard to do, with any kind of bulb, and some years I actually get around to it.

But in the garden, if I plant anything this fall, it will be little bulbs, particularly deep-blue scilla, and sky-blue chiondoxa (Glory of Snow). These do better in cold climates than warm. You can completely forget about them,

and they'll spread, so you can see why they appeal to me. I'll probably put some around the trees for a start, with some bone meal, and
hope that in a couple of years, I'll be able to move clumps of bulb-
laden sod to other spots in the garden. If you're going to try this, get
lots; when they're small, a hundred bulbs are only a joke. And if you
can get them to naturalize in the grass, which I particularly like,
remember not to mow until the foliage is completely brown. My grass
is slow in the spring, so I don't see that being a problem if I'm ever
lucky enough to have swathes of blue in my "lawn" to begin with.

Just don't think of bulbs as only the standard tall red tulips (usually
Darwins) or yellow daffodils (usually King Arthurs). There are hundreds if not thousands of other varieties and colours that bloom early,
mid-season, and late. But the leaving the foliage rule applies to all of
them. With daffodils and narcissi, you can tie the spiky leaves in a
knot, or roll them down and fasten with elastic to make them less
obtrusive. I used to do that, but then a helper I had once asked me if
I came out in the spring and untied them all, and suddenly it all
seemed too silly to bother with.

Of course it's not silly if you want to do it; nothing you do in the
garden is silly if it nourishes your spirit. But if you're more of a gin-
and-tonic gardener, I'd say read up on naturalizing.

Not Everything Works

I'VE REMEMBERED ANOTHER MUST-HAVE FOR MY GARDEN: a Pee Gee hydrangea shrub. Of course the reason I'm thinking of it now is because this is the time of the year when the Pee Gee is in its glory. There's one at the bottom of my street that must be twelve feet high, and is just covered with large mound-shaped clusters of flowers. It's about the only bloomer this late in the year. It starts around mid-August, and the creamy white blooms last a long time, slowly turning pinkish, then light brownish. That in itself makes it a very worthwhile shrub, but the big bonus is that the flowers last almost forever. Once you bring them in the house, they just slowly dry, right in the vase, maintaining whatever colour they had when you brought them in. Right now, I have a footed brass bowl of hydrangea looking positively luxurious on my coffee table, compliments of the woman down the street, and my being bold enough to knock on her door and ask her for a bunch. You can mix them with other dried flowers, or even silks. I think I'll add some ivy to mine, but they really don't need a thing.

"They" say Pee Gee hydrangea will root very quickly, and produce blooms when it's still not much more than a cutting, and that the colour of the blooms can be changed by adding stuff to the soil; aluminum sulphate will turn them blue! I haven't tried either but that's what "they" say.

The big debate with me now (crucial, even though I'm debating with myself), is whether to transplant wild stuff now, or wait. I've been advised by a local nurseryman to put it off until spring. He says in our climate, you should mark what you want in the fall, and move it early in the spring because your greatest chance of success is if the plant is dormant. If you wait until it's dormant in the fall to move it, it won't have time to make good roots before the weather gets bad.

Good advice I guess, but getting at it early enough in the spring before it breaks dormancy is hard to do when you're not ready to break dormancy yourself. Maybe I'll get all the ground ready this fall, move some now, and some more in the spring—just to cover my bets.

Speaking of getting the ground ready, I haven't had my soil tested, but I think it must be missing something. Yesterday I went to the cemetery and was astounded at how much the rose I planted for my mother has grown. It bloomed earlier in the summer, and now has thirteen big buds, and is at least twice the size it was when I planted it! I haven't fed it, or fussed over it at all, and it's done much better, in poorer-looking soil, than the ones I planted in my garden.

In fact, as I look around, the Virginia creeper and day lilies don't seem to have grown as much as I thought they would, and my cosmos didn't do well at all.

My soil looks and feels good, but I think I will get it tested. My first summer gardening in this location hasn't produced anything remarkable, but I have done a lot of work by my standards. I want all the help I can get, and the more work your soil does, the less you have to do to get things to grow.

I've had some good feeds of yellow beans, but so did the slugs. The Scarlet Runners I planted late still aren't ready to eat, but they sure are pretty. The few tomatoes ripening on the plant a friend gave me have been almost obscured by climbing nasturtiums. My perennial seeds still are not doing well, probably because we've had so much rain over the past four weeks. They're up, but not growing, and I'm starting to remember why I swore off gardening a few years ago.

Of course as soon as the sun shines and something I planted pleasantly surprises me, I'll forget again.

A Rose Is a Rose Is Not a Turnip

I HAD FRIENDS STAY FOR SUPPER THE OTHER DAY. I served pasta, hot rolls, and Greek salad. My pasta contained parsley, chives, and oregano from my garden, and the tomatoes in the salad were also picked by my own hands. It was a really good meal, thrown together quickly for unexpected company.

And yet I was a wee bit ashamed— and just when I thought I was cured!

Do you remember when I took up gardening again this spring, how determined I was not to become a slave to it; to keep the upper hand, and remember to stop and smell the roses? I did a really good job of that, even though I also accomplished a lot in the garden.

But not quite enough! I forgot the time of the year when gin-and-tonic gardeners are at our most vulnerable—this time of the year—harvest time! I forgot that you have to have a party piece in your garden; something you can put on the table to divert attention from all the stuff you don't have.

I had my own calendulas and nasturtiums for a centrepiece and even a very nice wine of my own vintage. Not enough!

Come September, you have to have one thing really special or you're exposed, defenceless. Next year, I'm going to aim for bowls of roses. If I had bowls of roses in the house, I wouldn't be daunted by talk of other dinners where they had corn just picked while the water boiled. I could serenely bend and inhale the scent, when the conversation turned to tomato slices that covered a side plate; dreamily rub a fallen petal against my cheek when yields of pickling cucumbers are compared.

The idea is to give the impression that you're so enchanted and preoccupied by whatever it is you've chosen for your party piece, that everything else is mundane. You smile absentmindedly at tales of "my zucchini is bigger than your zucchini" unless of course, zucchini is what you've chosen. Which is not a bad idea; they are prolific. Finding ways to use them up can become a challenge, though, and friends may start avoiding you on the street. On the other hand, you may make new friends when you start giving them away to strangers!

Now's the time to plan your strategy for next year. Look around at what everybody else in your circle has, and then think about something different that you could be good at. If nothing springs to mind, then do some research. There's only one main criterion: you have to be able to show it off in early fall. The peonies that were so fabulous in June will do you no good at all this time of the year.

Of course edibles are the stars at harvest time, and next year, I will plant more veggies, just because I want to. But let's face it; right now you can get wonderful fresh bounty at wonderful prices from markets and roadside vendors at every turn. You can also get an amazing variety of cut flowers, but never have I seen bouquets of garden roses for sale.

Roses have a mystique. How could a prize-turnip grower brag in the face of roses? As long as you grow roses, you don't have to apologize for anything, and you can show off for months. One perfect rose in July will ward off the early lettuce crowd like garlic will a vampire.

I'm away and dreaming about next year. With all the rain we've been getting, I haven't been able to do much else, garden-wise. A few more nice sunny days shouldn't be too much to ask for, to do a bit of cleanup, and get the garden (and the gardener) ready for winter.

Marigolds and Wildflowers

THE GARDENING ACQUAINTANCE WHO I CALL MARIGOLD brought me some broccoli. Lovely and firm, smallish heads; side shoots from the main heads she harvested weeks ago. She'll be picking them right up until December, she told me.

I don't know her well, but I don't feel a bit of remorse for calling her Marigold in my head because her garden is very sturdy and upright. She brought me the broccoli to be friendly and, "because I've seen you working away in the garden and have been dying to see what you've been doing." Then she said, standing on my front steps, "It's looking so much nicer than it used to, but I guess you've done most of your work in the back!" She was right of course, because of the tub and patio project. But the hammock also had a lot to do with all the time I spent in the back.

I immediately didn't want to show it to her. She couldn't see my back yard from outside unless she climbed the bank by the road, but I've seen the perfectly geometrical beds on her level property, formally centred with standards, every thing laid out in rows. I knew she was expecting to see more actually growing in my back yard than there was, for all the time I'd spent out there, and no matter how you try and stretch it, yellow and Scarlet Runner beans, snow-in-summer, day lilies, seedlings, and two lilac trees does not a summer's work make.

There was no way out of it, though, because after all, we're both gardeners, and so the tour began. She pronounced me clever for the bathtub/pool, refrained from mentioning my not-really-level patio, and said my mound had a lot of potential. Stopping by the log-bordered herb bed by the back door, rampant with climbing nasturtiums, she remarked how quickly it will all get away from you in a tangle if you don't stay right on top of it. When I told her I kind of liked things to get away from me and do their own thing, she laughed as if I was joking. I was starting to feel a little defensive and hoping she'd never find out I write a gardening column, when bless her, she invited me over for a closer look at her place.

I was so right when I nicknamed her Marigold, although I hope she never finds that out either! Neat wax begonias, and yes, marigolds, in blocks of nine, perfectly clumped perennials, everything mulched, not a weed in sight. I actually liked it better from the road because distance blurred the absolute boredom of it. Suddenly, instead of feeling apologetic about my casual patch, I felt a bit sorry for this nice woman. I'm sure keeping the garden beds tidy is as routine to her as changing the sheets on the beds, or cleaning out the bathroom.

(Neither of which is perfectly timed routine to me, if I'm being perfectly honest.)

The giveaway was in the way she talked about the garden. Not with any joy about the scents or colours, no affectionate stories, but all about how well behaved this or that was. She had nothing that sprawled or popped up where it wasn't expected. Her pleasure in this garden was in presenting a respectable face to the world. I'll bet her kids never went off to school with a button missing or a peanut-butter stain. I suppose there's a joy in seeing everything in perfect order, but I can't help but feel that Mother Nature likes me better, even if she does wish I wasn't quite so slack sometimes.

This is the time of the year when I make lots of garden promises to myself for next year. Making lots is a good idea, because then I usually manage to keep a few. In reality, this is identity crisis time for me.

My mind starts to thinks like a serious gardener, but my body is already leaning towards the fire. And on this Thanksgiving, while I'm promising myself that next year I'll have more bounty from my own garden on the table, I'll secretly give thanks that Mother Nature created me as a more of a wildflower than a marigold.

What to Do When Your Baby Goes Bad

THIS WEEK MARTHA-WOMEN ARE PROBABLY making dill pickles and harvesting the last of the herbs for drying. Instead of being caught up in the joys of Nature's bounty, I'm sitting here eating chocolate and drinking the brandy I bought for the cherries I didn't get around to bottling.

I do have a few things to harvest, a few herbs I could freeze-dry, but instead, I am somewhat distracted as I sit here, holding a tiny, still warm, body in my hands while the killer brazenly licks his chops, and stares at me resentfully for spoiling his fun.

I am harbouring a serial killer, and worse, I've been covering up for him. I've disposed of the bodies, and, God help me, first when it started, I even praised him. Bushka, my cat, has enjoyed many an hour this summer, in the tall, unmowed, meadowy stuff growing in what used to be the raised vegetable bed. I've rather enjoyed watching him, motionless, staring at some little field mouse my eye can't see, tail twitching, and then springing. He's never actually caught anything while I've been watching, and I've been so pleased that I left that wild patch for him to play hunting in.

But this is the time of the year when little field mice start thinking about coming indoors for the winter. "Good Bushka, you'll keep Mom's house mouse free," I crooned one morning, as he proudly laid a wee grey four-legged critter on the doorstep.

"That's a good sign," Daughter #1 told me, "that he brings his kill home to you." And I believed her, and kept praising Bush until I found him tossing one seemingly dead mouse up in the air, and realized that those little squeaks weren't coming from me.

It got worse. I got up one morning to a pile of feathers on the floor outside my bedroom door. As of today the count is up to two yellow

warblers, one purple finch, one black-capped chickadee, and two small wrens. Identifying the bodies is giving a macabre new use to my *Audubon Society Field Guide*.

Of course I didn't praise him for bringing me the birds. I was horrified and scolded him soundly, so then I caught him trying to hide one under my bed. He is an extraordinarily smart cat. He opens the bedroom door by jumping off the bed onto the door knob. He even operates the fax machine (I kid you not). This morning when I saw him jumping for the cord of the blinds in the front window, I figured he just wanted to have a look outside. Then I found a little bird cowering in the corner. That one I rescued, but I wasn't around for the one I found him with under the coffee table an hour later.

I really like watching birds. I think of them when I'm deciding what to plant. I have feeders. But I'm also pretty attached to Bush. For him to hunt is in the order of nature, and I don't believe in punishing him for doing what Nature intended, but I can't keep luring birds in to die.

Martha-women would probably have lots of cute solutions (and start saving feathers for Christmas crafts). Me, I guess I'll just put a bell on the cat, and try to be more understanding of women who appear on those "I Know He's Bad, But I Love Him Anyway" talk shows.

Before You Hibernate...

WHEN THE WEATHER STARTS TO KEEP ME OUT OF THE GARDEN, I find myself reading more gardening stuff. Even though I've moved five times in the past five years, I still have gardening magazines from the eighties, kept for one article or another. Every now and then, I cull through a few and cut out the pieces I want to keep, in theory keeping the size of the stack under control.

I should do that with every one, to save myself from what I've been doing this week; looking in vain for an article on firepits that I know is in the pile somewhere.

I don't need the article to convince me of the joys of having a firepit in your garden. I guess I don't really need it to help me build one, but I always like to read as much as I can about other people's experiences with something that interests me.

And firepits interest me. Before next fall, I want to have one! Given the number of cool nights we have, even in the midst of the growing season, a firepit should get more use, and give more comfort, than any swimming pool. Of course you don't have to build it yourself anymore since they've finally came out with portable ones. A fire-loving friend has a metal one on his deck. He put a piece of sheet metal under it, which heats up just enough to warm your toes, and can be nicely camouflaged with high-heat paint.

What a great thing, at this time of the year, to be able to sit around on your deck and drink hot chocolate laced with black rum around a toasty fire. Autumn nights are different altogether from summer nights. Crisper, clearer, even the smells are different.

In my childhood, burning leaves was one of the smells of autumn. In F.L., I had so many birch and maple trees that I used to give bags of leaves away and still have lots for compost.

Now I'm the one begging leaves for compost. Piles of leaves left by themselves in the fall will just be wet piles in the spring. You can bury them deep in beds, but they make a great addition to the compost pile. I just keep them in bags and add them in the spring and summer.

Once I read an article on making cold-climate compost all winter. It started off by saying you needed to build a pile that was twenty feet by twenty feet by ten feet to maintain heat. I think I stopped reading at that point. My Aunt Bessie used to chop kitchen clippings up in her blender all winter long and keep them in buckets out back. She had a great little garden, and would never burn a leaf.

Leaves can also be used as mulch on perennials, but they are hard to remove in the early spring, especially if you have bulbs coming up through them. My mother often used spruce boughs to protect her perennials, and her roses, once she had hilled the roses up, with extra soil, not the soil they were growing in. And that's what I'll be doing with my roses. But not yet. Mine are finished for the season, but the yellow beauty on Mom's grave is still blooming, as if to remind me that she always hilled them up first, let the ground freeze, and then laid the boughs down to prevent the freezing and thawing cycle that is most ruinous to roses.

The idea with mulching most things for the winter is not to keep them from freezing, but to make sure they stay frozen until spring.

Oh, and if you find the idea of a firepit appealing, don't place it close enough to affect nearby plants going into dormancy. You may not want to be frozen, but they do.

Maybe Next Year

THERE'S SOMETHING VERY COTTAGEY AND COZY about window boxes. I love them even though I don't have any right now. I did go as far as to get some rough lumber and hand pick some interesting spruce slabs to make boxes under the three windows along the side of my garage, but of course I haven't gotten around to making them yet.

My love affair with window boxes began when I honeymooned in Austria, and lasted longer than the marriage. From the tiniest hut in the Alps to the great hotels of Vienna, window boxes were every-where. The flowers of choice were red and pink geraniums, usually surrounded by Baltic ivy. The most humble structures were made proud by window boxes. "Why is she thinking about window boxes at this time of the year?" you might be asking yourself. Because as much as I love them all summer, it's this time of the year that I really wish I had window boxes to work with.

They're lovely in the summer of course, full of gorgeous cascading and trailing things. Like any containerized plants, you have to watch that they don't dry out, and like any plants anywhere, you'll get your best show out of them by deadheading and feeding regularly. But in the fall, when most garden things are starting to die back or fade, window boxes can be used for a whole new seasonal look.

Whenever I see window boxes at this time of year looking bedraggled with dried-up lobelia, and unidentifiable stuff, I itch to pull it all out and start over; which would be fine if the window boxes were mine, but could be awkward otherwise.

The thing is you don't have to have live stuff in window boxes for them to look great. When everything else is dead, or covered with snow, you can still have fun being creative in these mini-gardens.

Lots of stuff that you might use inside the house for autumn decorating will look just as good outside. Something as simple as bunches of red and gold autumn leaves poked into the soil of a window box can brighten up your garden, and your house, until you replace them with Christmas boughs. Branches with red dogwood berries, or orange bittersweet, or rose hips will all add colour while attracting birds. You could actually start with the evergreen boughs now as a base, and just change the fillers for fall, Halloween, Christmas, whatever. If you stick the boughs as deep as you can into the soil, they'll last for months until next spring. You might want to secure them with a few tent pegs and some wire against winter winds, or do what I usually do, just stick them back in again if they blow out. That's why I consider window boxes a bonus for fall and winter. But if you really need a garden fix, and want to do something different, you could also have window boxes inside the house.

I mean, where is it written that they have to be outdoors? It's just one of those things you never think about, but why not? Kathy Lee Gifford has them at her house (even though she probably has a gardener to look after them). With inside window boxes, you could have fresh flowers all year long, or even fresh salads. I guess. What you might grow inside is pretty much anything you might grow outside.

You could even use the same boxes, but I'd advise replacing the soil, and making sure they're bug free. I think I'd rather leave the outside ones for boughs and the like, and have matching ones inside the windows.

Inside window boxes—an ambitious thought for someone who hasn't gotten around to making up the outside ones yet!

A Gal's Gotta Do What a Gal's Gotta Do

THAT SUBTLE PRESSURE TO MOVE HAS BEEN LURKING. Leave Stephenville and head for the bright city lights. I can't deny the professional advantages, and there are good family reasons, so I've been thinking about it for a while, making up my mind, and then changing it every week or so.

My mind keeps going over the opening dialogue from the *Beverly Hillbillies*, where Jed asks Cousin Pearl if she thinks he should move just because he's discovered oil on his land. Pearl says, "Jed, look around ya. You're eight miles from your nearest neighbour, you're overrun with skunks, 'possums, and coyotes, you're cookin' on a wood stove summer and winter, your bathroom is fifty feet from your house, and you ask should you move?" and Jed says, "Yeah, reckon you're right Pearl. A man'd be a dang fool to leave all this."

I have no idea why I remember all that, but something subliminal makes me feel a strong bond with Jed Clampett.

I went down to my little fishing shack, a lifelong dream come true, on a stretch of beach just twenty minutes from my house. I sat outside on my weathered old breakwater, and watched an osprey dive for a fish. I looked at the gaps in the walls and thought about the work ahead to fix it up.

I thought about my bungalow back in Stephenville—kinda boring from the outside, with blue vinyl siding I hate, two years of work already gone into cozying up the inside and the past months in the garden.

But mostly I looked at the deep pink beach roses, and the mauve wild sweet peas tumbling over the old lobster pots, and thought about all my plans for the garden in Stephenville.

I'm a perennial type of gardener. That bungalow is the first house and garden I've owned all by myself. Everything I've dreamed and done back there was on the path of surrounding myself with plants and garden things that I love, and that speak to me in soft whispers.

That garden, though old, isn't filled with great old perennials and shrubs. But it's sunny and welcoming, and makes me feel like it's really happy to finally have an owner who will cherish it and help it blossom. I already love this garden because it gives me a lot of positive reinforcement. It's been starved for attention for so long, that even my casual approach is really welcome. It never makes me feel guilty about anything.

So, I had decided not to move, in no small part because leaving the garden would feel like a betrayal. Then this week came the final professional temptation, and fickle hussy that I am, I'm off to St. John's next month.

There's good news and bad news about the garden. The good news is that I'm renting the house, not selling it, so technically it's still my garden, and I can and will come back to it. The bad news is that the couple I'm renting it to isn't the least bit interested in gardening. The poor garden has lived with total indifference before, so I guess losing me won't come as too great a shock. It'll be interesting to see how the things I've planted survive on neglect, a trait that I consider very desirable anyway.

So it's not just the end of a season. When I pick up my pen next year, I'll be writing about a garden I haven't even met yet. I just hope it forgives me as much as this one has.

Starting Over

I'M SITTING HERE AT MY COMPUTER, looking out over my new backyard, starting to write about a whole new season of gin-and-tonic gardening. I confess to a lack of my usual enthusiasm, and I feel this will be very much a transition season for me.

I want to be in my house in Stephenville, going out every day to see what's come up, to thrill over how well this or that survived the winter. Instead, I'm in St. John's, with a very bare palette again. I could tell when I bought this property in November that the owners weren't gardeners, but the house, with a bathroom and bedroom on the main floor and an office upstairs, fills the needs of an eighty-six-year-old man and a wanna-be writer perfectly, A handful of yellow crocuses on a mossy bank last month gave me hope that maybe there were other surprises waiting to pop out and greet me of a spring morning.

I'm starting to doubt it. But as bare palettes go, this one does have a few interesting features. The house is a 1920s one-and-a-half storey, set on a steep hill in the west end of downtown St. John's. A central front dormer sits over a full-width verandah. Concrete steps and a path divide the front into two grassy squares. The up-street section is sloped. The down-street section is level because of a concrete retaining wall that drops six feet to a level driveway sloping all the way back to the rear fence. Beyond the house, the backyard is retained by much older-looking concrete sections. The yard climbs steeply up a ten-foot bank between me and the "up" neighbour. The "down" neighbour is an eight-foot drop from my driveway. Some attempt was made at terracing by a previous stalwart.

I have a yet unidentified smallish tree in the front, and five more somewhat larger ones along the back. An eight-foot wire fence follows the slope down to a new-looking tall green picket fence at the end of the driveway. The back has southern exposure, and, off the kitchen on the back upper side of the house, there's a nice deck on stilts towering above the garden. (Alas, there are no steps down to the garden.)

And so I wait. To see how the ground drains, how the sun hits different areas, how shady it will get when the trees leaf out.

All the moss (and the lack of sun on the deck so far) tells me at least one of the big trees will have to go. The wire fence is crying out for climbing, rambling, viney things; the tall green pickets are the perfect spot for sunflowers. The front must have a Pee Gee hydrangea, and I am tickled to finally have an old-fashioned covered verandah and a decent size deck to play with (and on).

And as I keep reminding myself, I haven't sold the house in Stephenville. A nice young family is renting it, and I can always go back and see how the garden is coming along, and take up any bits of stuff I want. Yup, I think I'll do exactly that in a month—or so.

I'm also remembering that things thrive on the east coast of Newfoundland that I never had much luck with on the western side of the island, and that I didn't have the space for on a balcony in Halifax, beautiful things like heathers and holly. So I must start observing, and talking to gardeners and nursery people.

And I must hit the yard sales with the verandah and deck in mind. Comfortable furniture is very crucial for sitting and contemplating what to do with the garden. I already have four rocking chairs of various vintage waiting for exterior treatment. What I really need is a rocking chair already weather-worthy to sit in while I contemplate what to do with the garden and all the other rocking chairs.

At least I still have my priorities straight.

The Cruelest Month

APRIL IS MY LEAST FAVOURITE TIME of the year as a gardener. At least in the dead of winter I know where I am; curled up by the fire, content with lovely gardening magazines and catalogues. But spring in our climate is totally unpredictable. One day it's warm and sunny and you get all in the mood, and rush out and buy garden stuff, and the next day the weather would break the heart of a stone.

How can I be old enough and wise enough to know that this is going to happen every year and yet still let it depress me? Yesterday was nice and sunny, and I was quite inspired. I potted up some begonia tubers and some dwarf nasturtium seeds, filled a glass of water with slips from a red coleus, and then went off to an auction. There I picked up a large oval enamel basin and a lovely urinal/bedpan combination in the same white enamel with blue trim. With a

matching chamber pot I picked up last week, it will make an interesting vignette of planters.

Today I planned to start digging. Even if you're not ready to plant you can get the soil ready, but gardening in the driving rain, high wind, and bitter cold is not my idea of fun. I guess that's part of what separates the gin-and-tonic gardeners from the "real" gardeners.

I picked up a pack of sunflower seeds by a Mr. Fothergill, called Allsorts: "an incredible assortment of colours and shapes from red to gold, lemon cream, and orange." Yesterday I bemoaned the fact that the ground by the back fence wasn't ready for seeds. Today I'm glad it wasn't. Who was it who said April is the cruelest month?

It's times like this that I miss having a greenhouse. I've had a couple over the years, made primarily from old windows. I hadn't thought about building one here, but now I'm remembering how nice it was to at least have a shed. On a day like this, back in Stephenville, I could get the big old round wood stove in the garage going, and start painting my verandah furniture.

I do have the perfect spot for a greenhouse. On the lower corner of this house, the basement is fully above ground, with a door opening onto a little flat spot with a southern exposure. Before I was a recovering compulsive gardener, I would have had something cobbled up there in no time. But now I know better. You see, the problem with having a little greenhouse is that it raises expectations. Yours and everybody else's! I've decided the pressure of having to produce is just not worth the pleasure of puttering around a greenhouse on a rainy day, as great as that is.

I'd just end up feeling guilty about possibly buying market tomatoes and lying about growing them to save face. You know those serious people who think greenhouses should be lush and full of wonderful things? They used to intimidate me, but now they make me a little hostile. I can see rackets starting over polite little remarks made about what's in my greenhouse. If I had one.

It's probably a good idea that I don't. Not when I still have other gardening issues to work through. I'm sure it's the weather that's making me so gloomy today. I hope it's not an omen of my gardening future in St. John's. The city certainly has its share of lovely gardens, but on a day like today, I fear maybe those gardeners are made of sterner stuff than I.

I think I'll light a fire and dig out some old magazines.

One Man's Shed Is Another Man's Cottage

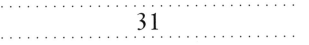

TWO FRIENDS HAVE ASKED ME FOR ADVICE on their gardens. Gwen almost doesn't know a rose from a rhubarb. Bob is actually a much more prolific grower than I am, but doesn't seem to have much imagination.

I first went to Bob's house for a fabulous Easter brunch buffet. He has a converted bedroom upstairs as a sort of conservatory; full of last year's geraniums, slips of this, cuttings of that, and lots of house plants. From this room we could see the backyard, a typical city lot; flat, fenced, trees along the back. Off to one side is a rectangular plot, vintage vegetable. On the other side is a long, white, somewhat scruffy, shed.

Bob thinks the garden will never look like anything as long as that shed is there, and bemoans the fact that he doesn't have a nice deck for entertaining because the shed is in the way. He barbecues in the driveway!

I think the shed is the best thing his garden has going for it. I covet that shed.

That shed could become a garden summer house. It would be the perfect hub for summer entertaining and gin-and-tonic gardening. Bob's father built the original eight-by-eight-foot structure around 1983. Over the next few years, he added two four-by-eight-foot pieces, all of the same wooden construction with clapboard exterior. It has one central door and one window at the end closest to the house. Right now it's crammed full of garden stuff, old sports stuff, and junk.

Bob could easily partition off a four-by-eight-foot area for storage (better organized storage), and have a lovely twelve-by-eight-foot space to play with and in, at far less than the cost of a new deck. In our climate, a summer house that you can open wide on a nice night, or close off on a not-so-nice night, would get a lot more use. Nice old windows and doors are not hard to find. I'd fill the front and the end with windows and screens, and scrounge a set of French doors somewhere. Even the un-handiest of men (which I think Bob may be) can put up trellises and lattice. Hanging pots and climbing things work wonders. Lattice, inside or out, can dis-

guise a multitude of sins.

There are few interiors that can't be cleaned up and covered with white paint. White paint can transform rough surfaces, yard-sale chairs, old wicker, almost anything, into summer house elements. Even if you keep the inside strictly as a potting and storage shed, there's no reason the outside of any structure that you have control over has to be an eyesore to your garden.

Gwen's new garden is large and flat, surrounded by a picket fence. It's an old-fashioned two-storey house on a bluff a few hundred yards back from the bay. In true outport tradition, the front garden, which faces the bay, is actually the back garden because everyone uses the back door for the front door. Therefore, the brick patio they plan to set in the grass in the front/back garden for the view will also have some privacy because nobody ever uses that door. That garden has four smallish willows planted in an L-shape, and two rugosa roses in front of a bay window. Gwen, not even a gin-and-tonic gardener, wants instant gratification, no maintenance, and doesn't want to spend much money starting off.

My advice to her was to keep the old-fashioned spirit of the garden. Do the hardscaping, and then spend her budget on trees, shrubs, and perennials in that order. She can always flesh it out with some annuals for fast colour, but plant some bones first.

I can tell by the way she nodded sagely that she has no intention of following my advice.

THE WEATHER HAS FINALLY CHANGED and I have had a relaxing, productive, fun gardening week. My windowsills on the south side are filled with the beginnings of my container gardening. Begonias are unfurling and nasturtiums are peeking through. I picked up some four-packs of sturdy pansies for only eighty-seven cents each. They just seemed perfect for the old enamel chamber pot I found, and I have a few left over for somewhere else.

I went out to investigate nurseries earlier in the week, and was surprised to find that most of them weren't really ready yet. I ended up at a department store where I was impressed by the quality of the shrubs and trees, and also by the prices.

My first find was a nested set of four salt-glazed earthen pots, in rich shades of terra cotta. They had just come in and were priced at $9.99, which the clerk mused might be a pricing error. Too bad, I thought, as I snapped up a set.

Then I started on a selection of shrubs that might prove irresistible to birds (I know, I know) and look good at the same time. First I chose a high bush cranberry, which I think I'll plant on the down-slope corner of the deck. At full height of twelve to fifteen feet, the top will be just about level with the railing. This shrub has flattish-topped white flowers and clusters of red berries, which should be interesting to look down on instead of the usual up at.

The steep bank on the upper side of the deck will be home to a Coral Beauty cotoneaster. Glossy, semi-evergreen foliage, and more red berries, but this time in ground cover. I've grown this little lovely before; it spreads nicely, and quickly.

My next choice was another cotoneaster, Peking. I've seen this as an unclipped hedge and loved it, but I bought only one. It has small black berries, but I would have bought it anyway because of the fall colour—a tapestry of crimson through bronze, copper, and gold.

After much deliberation, I couldn't resist a burning bush, for much the same reason. It's growing habit is sometimes a bit neat for my taste, but the scarlet of the papery thin leaves in the fall makes up for it being prissy. A bonus is the ridged wing-like effect on its branches, ethereal when lightly frosted with snow.

I just had to start on the wire fence because I won't be happy until it's totally disguised. I'm already making excuses for succumbing to a scarlet firethorn. I say succumbing because I'm not sure of its hardiness here. I was told this stock came from Nova Scotia, so hopefully it's not a big risk. Also, it's not called fire*thorn* for nothing.

Last, but definitely not least, I bought the very thing I had no intentions of buying: a hybrid tea rose. No way am I anywhere ready to think about, let alone start preparing for, hybrid teas. In fact I'd sworn off this fussiest of roses in favour of other varieties. But this is the Crimson Glory, my mother's favourite, that I tried to get last year, but couldn't. It has good thick stems and is just starting to bud out. Crimson Glory is an older rose. Mom got hers in the early fifties, and it died in the early nineties, just a few years before she did.

I remember the large dark blooms and the scent, heady, like roses are supposed to smell. Today I potted it up in the largest of my new pots, and I shall tend it lovingly on my sunny deck. If I remember cor-rectly, I won't even have to bend to enjoy the scent, but I will, probably every day, and I'll see my mother smiling as I do.

The pots are labelled frost resistant. I'll store Crimson Glory under the veranda, well covered, once it's dormant in the fall, and hope for the best.

Now that she's gone, on Mother's Day I am much more the child of my mother than I am the mother of my daughters. I think they'll understand when they have children of their own.

The Queen Mum and Other Hardy Perennials

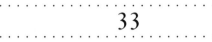

I REALLY LIKE THE QUEEN MUM. Not just because she is gracious and stayed in London during the Blitz, and all the other things that make Brits love her that I can't actually relate to personally. And not even because she loves gin and Dubonnet before lunch and a stiff martini before dinner, which I can relate to, even though I haven't yet succumbed to the lunch routine.

I like her because she is the personification of an older flower, and I think older flowers are wonderful. Older flowers are dependable. They don't demand fussing over. New varieties come out every year, but who knows what kind of staying power they will have. Maybe, generations from now, some of today's new varieties will join their ranks, but for now I'm drawn to the old standbys.

And even though I'm going low maintenance all the way, I've promised myself a rose garden. That's no longer a contradiction in terms. Older shrub varieties are now readily available, and newer shrub varieties, such as the David Austins and the Explorers, deliver wonderful old-fashioned blooms with much better resistance to hardship than their hybrid tea cousins.

Drive along rural roads. Often the only sign of families long gone is a spreading shrub rose. Around forgotten foundations, you'll find clumps of day lilies. Inside a tumbled down fence you'll spy a burst of scarlet peonies, or a stand of coreopsis.

It doesn't matter where you live (unless it's under snow year round) there are lovely old plants that will live happily in your garden, and make very few demands on you. And some of these will last a lot longer than you will.

Except for the trees, there's nothing much around my turn-of-the-century house to show anyone ever turned a spade of soil in the garden. When I go, I want people to know a gardener lived here. Not only that, I want them to know a gin-and-tonic gardener lived here. I want the garden I leave behind to survive without being fussed over. I want the spirit of serenity and relaxation to linger, as a welcome for my spirit, should it choose to visit.

It's nice if you have lasting garden structures as well as plants. And thanks to a garage sale last week, and an apartment being renovated, I have started on my collection.

At the garage sale I was thrilled to see two scarred old concrete lions, the type you see atop posts, even though I'm sure these are bigger. I'm not fond of them on posts, I suppose because I'm not keen on anything from nature looking too contrived, and you know lions would never perch on posts. These beauties, scars intact, are destined for the ground, maybe one will be hiding in long grass, waiting to pounce. They'd be wonderful too, guarding an arbour leading to the Queen Mum section of the garden, full of old-fashioned roses, elegant hollyhocks, and stately delphiniums. They were a bargain at fifty dollars for the pair, but because I figured it would cost me twenty dollars to get them home, I got them for twenty-five dollars. They're still waiting for me to find a couple of gorillas to go pick them up.

From the apartment, I rescued an old porcelain-covered, cast iron sink, complete with a drain board, that was on its way to the dump. I'm having a little déjà vu about the bathtub, but I haven't figured out yet how I'll use the sink. A water trough comes to mind, with something trickling, or a bird bath, or a planter. Inspiration will strike. In the meantime, I'll keep my eyes open for more architectural stuff. It makes for an interesting garden, and I have a feeling I'm going to need all the help I can get.

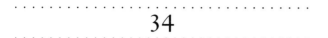

Of sun and shade

TAKING DOWN A TREE IS A BIG DECISION. Especially when you live in a city and have to justify that decision in order to get a permit to take down said tree. This is my first experience with such bureaucracy, and I wholeheartedly embrace the spirit of the regulation. Too many people are just too quick to cut down a century-old tree, just like too many are ready to tear down a lovely old building.

But I admit I hadn't even thought of having to get the approval of city hall before I called in the boys with the chainsaw. Now the city arborist is coming this week to make his/her call. I have six trees on my property in varying stages of maturity. I revere and respect trees. But I also have a definite soft spot for the feel of the evening sun on my body at the end of a day, and five of my six trees, along with four of my neighbour's, conspire to ensure that, once they all leaf out, southern exposure or not, my back deck will be deep in shade.

Horticulturally, I suppose could live with that because of all the wonderful shade-loving things I could grow there, even though I'd have to change my tastes some. Spiritually, I cannot. I have the front verandah for shade on a day that's too hot; the back deck I want for the warmth of the sun to warm my soul and my body, as well as my soil. Plus, the proximity of some of these trees means that none of them are doing well. My neighbour apparently has often bemoaned the fact that her lilacs don't get enough sun, so I think she'll be glad that I'm taking some action. Harmony in nature is all about balance, so don't be afraid to take down a tree or two in a good cause.

Because of this good cause, I've delayed planting the shrubs I bought. It seems to make more sense to see what the garden looks like when a tree or two are gone (not to mention keeping the shrubs out of harm's way). In the place of these large trees, I think I'll plant a medium-sized flowering crab, and a lilac. These won't shade the deck, but will give privacy from the back street below.

I'm investigating some interesting painting techniques for the concrete wall, pathway, and steps out front. I was wishing they were old stone, or brick, and then I had the brainwave that with all this faux painting on the go now, that look shouldn't be too hard to achieve. Flowers tumbling over concrete just doesn't have the same effect as tumbling over stone. I think I also want a picket fence of sorts, an archway, and a gate in the front. All of this should be done before any serious planting, so most of that will have to wait for the fall and next spring.

The small area in the front is reminiscent of tiny cottage garden space, and every morning, as I sip my coffee on the veranda, I look at it and think and plan. I note where the sun lies the longest. Sometimes I walk around the neighbouring downtown hills of St. John's, noticing what landscaping solutions others have come up with.

When I start planting the front, I will rent a sod turner and take up every blade of grass out there. The space is small, and mowing grass is a nuisance I can well do without. Despite the northern exposure, there is no end of ground covers and cottage plants to give me much more pleasure than grass.

By next week, I'll have a more specific plan for the front. Who knows, I might even have the "brickwork" finished.

Just a Little Out of Control

THE MOST EXCITING THING THAT'S HAPPENED TO ME this week is that I've discovered I have a lilac by my back fence. That is not an indication that I've had a boring week. In fact, on a personal level, my week has been rather interesting. However, tall, handsome men may come and go, but a nice bushy, four-foot lilac is here to stay. Therefore, sensibly, I give Lilac first place in my affection.

I knew, of course, that the shrub was there. I just didn't know it was a lilac until it leafed out. It has multiple branches from the base, somewhat thin. I'm sure it's of the common variety, *Syringa vulgaris*, and is a volunteer from next door. I don't think it's ever bloomed because Upper Neighbour didn't even know it was there. It was sort of obscured by low branches from a very sad-looking black ash, all of which I trimmed away as soon as I discovered Lilac. I've cleared away the drip line, top dressed it with sheep manure, and will pick up some more fertilizer this week. The suckers should transplant easily, so I'll also give that a try.

The day after I discovered Lilac and her offspring, the city arborist made his visit. After two months of studying the sun path, my trees, and my deck, I had no doubt about which trees had to go. Well, thanks to him, and also because of Lilac, the plan has changed again. He suggested extensive high pruning on the two big Norway maples I was going to remove, and removal of the ash and the scraggly maple next to it. I had already decided to sacrifice the ash to Lilac, but I hadn't really thought about pruning the big trees as an answer to letting more light in.

Also, by getting rid of two unattractive trees, I'll have room for something nicer, like forsythia, which I've added to my "must have" list. They were never very successful on the west coast of the island, but here in St. John's they are spectacular, as are rhododendrons, but somehow they're almost too spectacular for my taste. The whites or yellows may not be as bold, but the fuchsias are downright brazen. I just don't want anything screaming at me from the garden, even if it is in glorious beauty.

A lot of my shade comes from the trees next door. Upper Neighbour told me that her late husband planted them, and she can't bring herself to take any of them down, even though she, too, wishes she had less shade. That limited my sun options considerably, until I mentioned the pruning suggestion. She discussed it with her sons, who reckoned that their father would have wanted that done, and so that will help. There can be no harmony in a garden if there's no harmony with your next-door neighbour.

I've had a couple of estimates for the pruning, both for around a hundred dollars if they don't have to take all the branches away, which they won't, because I have a little bucksaw, a fireplace, and a secret yen to experiment with a twig arbour and some trellis. Another pleasant surprise—I've been told that the vine on the lattice under the deck is a honeysuckle. It appears to have at least four different root sections, so I should be able to move a couple to the wire fence in the back. It's almost like Christmas, waiting to see what kind of honeysuckle it is. It still has clusters of red berries from last year, which to me doesn't sound like a honeysuckle, but I don't know everything (!) As soon as the tree work is finished next week, I'll get at the job of covering up that fence.

A neighbour back in F.L. had a deep red Japanese quince espaliered on a chain-link fence. Although gorgeous for only a few weeks in the spring, I'd love to have one.

My list is threatening to get out of control!

But I'm not. Not yet.

JUNE

Outdoor Decor

THERE'S NO LAW THAT SAYS OUTDOOR FURNITURE has to be outdoor furniture. I mean, what did people do years ago before resin? Let's go way back, even before lightweight aluminum framing. The well-heeled may have had cast or wrought iron. Wicker was considered more suitable for covered verandas and sun porches. The rest of the masses, if they had any furniture outdoors at all, had wood. It was, and still is, simply a matter of a few coats of an exterior paint or stain, and any wooden piece can not only do duty on the deck, but look a lot better and have a lot more individuality, than white plastic.

When you have a big veranda, plus a deck, you will need a fair bit of stuff. I guess I should say, I will need a fair bit of stuff, because unfortunately I've never seen a space yet that I didn't want to fill. And I am not impressed with lugging furniture back and forth from one area to the other. Of course, ease of lugging is one advantage of modern resins and plastics. But if you just don't like the look of the cheap stuff, and can't afford the expensive stuff, then "real furniture" from the basement, yard sales, or second-hand stores is the answer.

Dad's chair on the front veranda is a pine glider rocker that came with the house in Stephenville. Mine is an old hardwood Lincoln rocker with lovely scrolled arms, sloping back and cane inserts. I found it in two pieces in a barn in Nova Scotia years ago. We each have a small wicker table for a cold drink, and under the window is a long wicker table for plants, the newspaper, whatever. This sturdy set of tables was a fifteen-dollar yard-sale purchase last year for Daughter #1's apartment. With a can of burgundy exterior spray paint, they are now stunning on the veranda. Some more exterior paint, and a couple of nice, fat, green-and-white striped, outdoor chair pads, and I have one side of my veranda furnished beautifully for morning coffee and cozy chats.

The back deck is taking a little longer to come together. I've been

looking, without success, for a cheap old wooden table to paint—cheap being the operative word. Now I've even taken a second look at a table I have in the basement with chrome legs and a simulated wood top. The design of the legs is such that I think a can of black spray paint, and some creativity for the top can make it look very wrought iron and old world. I have two small wooden rockers on the deck now. Just add some all-weather pads, and rockers are great for outdoors because they're reclined slightly and are more relaxing than stiffer chairs. As soon as I find a few more comfy pieces, we'll be all set for dining alfresco.

Another good thing to keep an eye out for is a small bureau, microwave cart, or some such piece that you can use for a serving surface. Drawers and shelves can store barbecue supplies, outdoor dishes, napkins and the like. Putting casters on the bottom is a nice touch so you can move it around easily. Old metal furniture, the kind you used to find in institutions, and on military bases, is great for outdoor adaptation, and rust proof paint comes in all sorts of colours. Why carry everything back and forth from the house every time you feel like eating outdoors?

A big old trunk can double as extra seating, and storage for cushions and stuff. A fresh "aged" coat of paint has turned a kitchen chair with a nice back and a broken seat into an attractive plant stand. With exterior paint you can bring lots of original indoor things, like shelving units, to your outdoor space. There's something kind of homey about it, and you have more money for little treats, like steak instead of hamburger, and a bit of gin for your lemonade. Now that's a good thing.

Right on the Line

I CONFESS THAT I AM VERY THANKFUL THAT FEW PEOPLE who read my column know where I live. My garden is just a neglect or two away from becoming a neighbourhood disgrace.

I've been putting things off in the garden for two weeks now because one little neglect leads to another. I neglected to put the phone number of Larry (?), the garden guy who's supposed to thin out some of my trees, in a safe place. Or else I put it in a safe place and that's why I now can't find it. Therefore my grass is now too high to cut with a lawn mower. Why you may ask?

Because I don't have a lawn mower, and neglected to do anything about the grass because I was going to get Larry to do it when he came to do the trees. Then I went away for three days, and dropped in on my Stephenville property to dig up some plants, and to get two wrought iron chairs and an arched wicker shelving unit for my deck. However, I neglected to take my little red book with the tenants' phone number in it, so I couldn't call them to let them know I was coming. Naturally, they weren't home. I dug up some plants anyway, because we had talked about that before, but the garage was locked, so all I could do was gaze woefully in the window at the desired furniture neatly stored up in the rafters, and at the pots I had planned to put said uprooted plants in. I managed with small grocery bags, but neglected to bring some plastic to protect the floor of the van, and therefore couldn't give the plants very much water. Then we drove across the island on a twenty-nine-degree day with no air conditioning. When I arrived home at midnight, I didn't take the plants out of my friend's van because I was so tired, but he assured me he'd be by with them first thing in the morning, before his 9:30 appointment.

Well, he either forgot to get up in time, or hasn't noticed that his van is quickly becoming a plant hearse, because it's now noon, and I still haven't seen the sky over Aunt Gladys's snow-in-summer or Sheila's achillea. I'm in the horrors. Things in the garden seem so out of control that I wouldn't even be able to enjoy a gin and tonic outdoors now. And that is pretty bad!

The garden in Stephenville seems indifferent to neglect. Maybe there's a message there. Nothing has been fed, pruned, or divided, but it looks ok.

Climbing Don Juan is still languishing though. I considered digging him up because he's in a vulnerable spot for the lawn mower if his base isn't kept clear, and it probably won't be. But I left him there. For some reason I have no affection for him. It's totally irrational, but I know in my heart it has to do with that "fussy male who needs to be looked after" thing. Don Juan will either prove himself tough enough to survive on his own, charm someone else into taking care of him, or fall into decline. If he's still there next year, I'll consider him worthy of my attention.

I've been making some calls. I've found out that Larry the gardener is Harry the gardener. That's a start. Whether I find him, or get someone else, the push is on this week. There's a fine line between being a relaxed gardener (a good thing) and being a slob (not a good thing).

38

Bonsai and Beaver Cove

HONEST GARDENING COLUMNIST THAT I AM, I feel duty bound to report my failures. Besides, if I was one of those types who did everything right, most of you wouldn't like me half as much. Plus there's something to be said for learning what not to do.

Like plant pansies right in your chamber pot. I know, I know; container gardeners everywhere are crying, "Say it isn't so." Well it is, so accept it.

I put the recommended layer of stones in the bottom of my enamel pot and used a standard potting mixture. Pansies seemed to fit the look, and they were quite perky at first. Then we had some heavy rain, and they became somewhat waterlogged. I wasn't too concerned; the next few days of sun would dry things out. I suppose I should have paid more attention, because the next time I looked, it was too late. The poor little things had drowned, rotted right away. So now the chamber pot holds another pot, a plastic flower pot, which can be lifted out and excess water poured off. Not exactly rocket science, but

I just happen to like the look of things planted directly in unusual containers. I've never had a soggy problem before. Maybe the karma of this particular container predisposed it to water retention.

Speaking of containers, last week I visited a rooftop garden here in St. John's. What a spot for sun, the fourth floor of an old Water Street building. No problem here with too much shade.

The owner, a man of many experiences, is, however, a self-confessed novice gardener. But he has made a start with some half barrels. One holds a grapevine, planted last year and looking good after being left unprotected all winter. Another holds a very Charlie Brown–looking larch (or juniper). My host looked at that one as a bit of a failure, and I could see why, but I looked at it and thought bonsai! Big bonsai.

Bonsai is the oriental art of cultivating normally large trees as miniatures in containers. Art is the operative word here. Bonsai is one of those things I've been planning to take up sometime, and this juniper seemed to whisper soft words in Japanese to me. Saki, saki.

Some careful pruning (my very favourite garden task), some wiring, a small piece of statuary, and Clyde would not only have a beautiful conversation piece, but would even manage to convince people that that was what he had planned all along.

I couldn't resist picking up a cast iron pagoda-style lantern on sale at a department store, just to inspire him. Not selflessly of course. I'm dying to be part of the process. I'll drop off the lantern with my *Create Your Own Bonsai* by Ken Norman, and a note offering to bring my own cutters, and sit back and wait for the invitation.

Just the thought of it inspired me. I came home and planted a six-inch spruce seedling in a shallow pocket of the piece of driftwood that sits on my deck. It could make a stunning bonsai, but I know I'll have to enlarge the planting pocket a bit. When I'm at my desk in the garret now I can look down on it, and it already gives me pleasure.

I'm not inspired with much else. In fact, I'm yearning for Nova Scotia this week. I don't quite know why; I love Newfoundland. But I want to see the day lilies blooming on the side of the road on the South Shore, and the lupins in Cape Breton. My heart wanders back to smelling the apple blossoms while hanging clothes in Beaver Cove, or putting up lattice on my balcony in Halifax, and I'm strangely sad.

I'm shamelessly looking for a professional reason to justify a trip over there, and am open to any suggestions.

39

Find Your Garden's Spirit

REMEMBER BOB AND GWEN, my two friends who asked me for advice on their gardens? Bob has the shady urban backyard with an ugly shed. Gwen has a sunny outport garden, on an exposed rise just back from a windy headland.

Gwen has known me since we were fifteen. So far she hasn't taken any of my advice. Bob has known only me for a couple of years. He's jumping in with a vengeance. I am choosing not to dwell on the subliminal message there.

Gwen gave me money a few weeks back to pick up some shrubs for her. I bought a nice fat Bristol Ruby weigela, in glorious bud (to satisfy her need for instant gratification), and two very nice container shrub roses. One was an Explorer, and the other a rugosa. There wasn't a lot to choose from, but it still took me about a half-an-hour to decide on the very best specimens for her garden.

She loved the weigela, but I didn't get the same enthusiasm for the roses, even though I explained what they would be like and why I had picked them. A week later she confessed she had taken them back. "I hope you don't mind, but I don't think I'd like anything as formal as rose bushes." To Gwen, the word rose conjured up visions of long-stemmed hybrid teas (even though she doesn't know that's what they're called). Everything I said about the ones I had chosen, and why, went in one ear and out the other. In place of the roses she got potentilla, and then announced she'd rather grow vegetables anyway. Potentilla is hardy and produces lots of little flowers. It's one of those shrubs landscapers call "useful." I find it sort of insipid, boring actually. So I'm washing my hands of Gwen's garden for now.

Bob, on the other hand, loved my idea of turning his large shed into a summer house. He also planted a lovely rectangular bed of veggies, which he didn't ask me anything about. And why should he? This is something he's been doing for a few years, his father did before him in the same piece of ground, and he's very comfortable with it.

And that's the way it should be.

All the therapists will tell you how important it is to be comfortable in your own skin—to like yourself. If you don't like yourself, you should make some changes. It's the same with gardens. If you feel really good about your garden, don't change it just to suit somebody else's idea of what a garden should be. But, if your "good" feeling is defensiveness in disguise, step back and have a look. This is your property. Don't be intimidated by anything the neighbours or in-laws have to say. Your home is your castle, therefore your piece of land is your castle ground.

I don't much like my castle ground right now. But I do feel good about what I've done to improve it since I moved in only six months ago.

Bob grew up in the house he now owns. His father and mother set the pattern of the front and back yards. He has pretty much followed that pattern. Perhaps had I suggested sweeping changes to the horticultural side of things, it might not have been as well received. But because the major change is hardscaping—architectural and practical—it captures his imagination without intimidating his pale green thumb.

The thing is a garden may have a personality or a past. Some old gardens have a spirit. It would be nice if you found it or at least recognized that it exists. And remember that in a new garden, whatever you do helps create the spirit.

The important thing is that you and your garden like each other. I'm working on mine.

. . . .
40
. . . .

JULY

Excuses, Excuses

YOU KNOW THAT STAGE WHEN YOU'RE letting your hair grow out, and it looks like nothing on earth, and it's driving you crazy and you want to go around with a paper bag over your head or a sign around your neck explaining why you look like this?

I'm kind of like that right now with the garden. It's not because I'm waiting for things to grow. It's worse than that. I'm waiting to get some outside refurbishing done and first things have to come first, or else you waste a lot of time and energy, not to mention money. How big a masochist would I have to be to dig and plant in the front yard knowing that it will soon be full of men and ladders and stuff, helping me fix the verandah and front steps and build a fence?

What kind of a glutton for punishment would plant one more thing in the backyard, having decided that she cannot live without steps built down from the deck, despite earlier resolve?

I know what I want in this new garden, and it's in perfect harmony with the style and spirit of this turn-of-the-century storey-and-a-half house. I see a cottage-style flower garden, lots of old-fashioned shrub roses, a bird garden in the back, and ground cover in the front. I am making some progress, but much too much of it hasn't yet made its way out of my head onto the land.

Part of the reason is that I just don't seem to have it in me to turn mean ground anymore. I make no excuses or apologies. It's not my fault the ground is mean; I just got here. So I'm resentful, and maybe I'm sulking a bit.

But while I'm sucking my thumb, I'm consoled by the knowledge that waiting is the right thing to do. I expect the construction work will all be done by August, and there'll still be lots of time to put in perennials and shrubs, and get them well established for next year.

And there are financial advantages to doing the garden this way. You can pick up a container plant or two every week over the summer less painfully (on the wallet) than buying them all at once. Later in the season, you'll find more bargains, and you can start perennial and biennial seeds in flats or pots to be ready for next year's blooms.

The drawback with having everything in containers waiting for the garden to be ready is that you have to be very vigilant with the watering. If you let them really dry out, it makes watering more difficult. I have two fuchsias on the veranda. One gets more sun than the other, and dried out before I realized it. Now the water just runs through it. The only way to rectify this is to put the container down in water for a few hours and let the water really soak through.

And so I putz around, planting things up in pots, making jokes with the neighbours about how they're putting me to shame. It's even a challenge to enjoy my evening gin and tonic guilt free while I'm in this particular slump, but I'm giving it my best shot.

Maybe I'm getting too good at it. The other day, I found myself humming David Frizzell's "I'm Gonna Hire a Wino" (a country classic for those of you who don't share my eclectic taste in music). New lyrics just came to me unbidden:

I'm gonna hire a helper
To till and plant my yard
So I'll feel more at rest there
And won't have to work so hard!
I'll take out the grass on the front lawn,
Train ivy to hide the wall,
And won't plant things like dahlias
To torment me in the fall.

The sooner I get that carpenter in here the better!

. . . .

41

. . . .

More Than
One Kind of Spirits

YOU KNOW I'M THE FIRST TO ADMIT THAT I don't have a gardening-magazine type of garden. This year that's an understatement.

Now some gardeners might say that it's because I don't take it seriously enough. I don't pay enough attention to the feeding and the pests and all that stuff. Which may be true, but the reason I prefer (and you can use this too, even if you don't really believe it like I do), is that I have a more spiritual relationship with my plants.

When I put a plant or a seed in the ground, I feel like I've done a good thing for it and it should respond in kind. I used to keep this unorthodox philosophy to myself, but now I make no excuses for having the kind of garden where Mother Nature makes most of the decisions.

And it's worked for me until now. I've had good relationships with my gardens. I've enjoyed them even if they've never reached show-place status.

But even I know about the futility of tossing seed onto fallow ground. My ground makes fallow look good. Early in the season, I bought some bags of compost and sheep manure, but if I had to buy all I could use, I'd have to take out a second mortgage on the house.

Everything I planted this year is at least surviving. The best thing I can do for the rest of the season is start collecting stuff for the soil. There's no reason I can't accumulate a few garbage bags full every week. Gathering seaweed is the perfect excuse for a trip to the seaside (as if I needed an excuse). Weekend drives along country yard-sale routes lead to lots of manure sources. The caplin are rolling in Middle Cove, and whatever I can get (over and above what Dad can eat) will go into the garden (dug deep of course). Grass clippings will be bagged and in the fall I'll have leaves. Nothing compostable will ever be thrown out again. The big soil drive is on. There's not too much we can expect from the garden spirits if we neglect the soil. If I make the earth as healthy as I can, the inhabitants of my garden will be strong without a lot of extra fussing from me.

Right now even my nasturtiums are conspiring against me. Nasturtiums are one of the few plants that don't like rich soil. They actually like poor soil. Naturally, I've relied on them for years. But I've never grown them in a container before. Back in April, I filled my pot with commercial potting soil, like you would, and popped in my seeds. I've been waiting for blooms ever since.

The foliage is fantastic. And each day that I peer among it looking for buds, I remember hearing my mother giggling. Mom was one of the local gardening divas, and a man in our old neighbourhood called her over to brag about the size of his nasturtium leaves. "He won't get one flower," she predicted. "Imagine fertilizing nasturtiums!" Which of course makes them perfect for me, and is probably why I've remembered that story for decades.

I must have stumbled on some very nutritious potting soil. I wish I could remember what kind it was. I'd almost given up hope, and then yesterday, I discovered a few tiny buds. Maybe the nutrients are all used up now, and I'll get blooms for the rest of the season.

Sometimes it seems like the only good spirits in my garden this year are the kind that go well with a slice of lemon. But even they'll taste better when everything else is in harmony, so I'll remember to throw the lemon rind in the compost.

Wild Thing

I'M JUST NOT SATISFIED AT HOME, so I have begun seeking my pleasure elsewhere. That might sound drastic, but before you sic Dr. Ruth on me, consider just how deprived I am. Horticulturally speaking, of course.

For me, one of the best reasons to garden is so I can have great bunches of fresh flowers in the house. My garden just can't deliver the goods this year, what with being somewhat of a "garden-in-waiting" and all.

So I've taken to wandering, walking on the wild side, you might say.

I thought I was fairly well informed, but I had no idea just how many different kinds of wild-flowers are out there! Maybe because I'm flower starved myself,

I've just become more aware, but there seem to be blossoms mocking me everywhere I turn.

Suddenly, I'm all agog with a whole new world of flowers. I had to rush out and buy a book to brush up on this treasure trove. I also keep thinking about Walter Ostrom's garden on the rocky shores of Indian Harbour, just south of Halifax. I visited and wrote about this very special garden for *Canadian Gardening* years ago. I don't even know if Walter and Elaine are still there, but I'm sure the garden will endure forever because Walter filled it with native plants and their foreign or domestic relatives.

It's such a simple, logical concept for gardening, yet one that most of us don't readily think of.

Right now I'm content just to help myself to some of the flowers, but every time I go out I see wonderful specimens that I think I'd like to have in my garden. I haven't had much experience in transplanting from the wild. Obviously this wouldn't be the best time, but this is a good time to mark the ones you want, because they'll look different in the fall and spring. There are a few species that are protected, and others that don't transplant well, so a little research about your neck of the woods is a good idea.

There are many cultivated families with wild relatives (just ask some of my clan). Or maybe it's the other way around. One of my favourites is the beach pea (*Lathyrus japonicus*). Its perennial cousin, *Lathyrus latifolia*, is a lot easier to grow than the annual sweet pea. It tolerates poor, dry soil just like its beach relative. Neither of these hardy perennials have the range of colours that the annuals have, but they're a lot less fussy.

Daisies, asters, roses, rhododendrons, irises, primroses, forget-me-nots, mallows, and yarrows are just a few of the more common flowers that can be found growing wild on the other side of the fence, and enticed into the garden.

At the very least you can enjoy a bunch in the middle of your kitchen table. They look just as good, or better, in an enamel jug than a crystal vase, so in that sense they're more suitable for most of us. Add some grasses or fern, maybe a small piece of driftwood, and even Martha Stewart would call it a good thing. A friend of mine has some beautifully shaped, thick evergreens transplanted from the wild. Her secret is to plant three together, and prune the candles (new growth) hard each spring. Now you can't even tell that they're three trees instead of one, and they look like the perfect specimens you usually find only in pictures. If you are going to pick or transplant from the wild, do it with the same care you'd want someone else to show in your garden, because the wild garden belongs to all of us.

Oldie
but Goodie

MY GRANDMOTHER USED TO HAVE MULTICOLOURED house plants that she called "coolies." I'm sure she had others, but I remember only the coolies, probably because they were so colourful. They sort of went out of style for a long time, but like polyester pants, they are making a comeback. And why not? Heritage colours are in; heritage house plants can't be far behind.

Grammy's coolies are today's coleus, and coleus is making even

more of a splash now as a bedding plant for shady areas. They're grown for their foliage, not for a flower. In fact you should pinch off the insignificant flower to keep the plant full. The colours of the leaves can be almost startling: burgundy and lime, corals, reds, yellows, greens, and any combination thereof. I've never seen quite so many of them as I'm seeing this year at the garden centres, and I just succumbed to some for my veranda.

What younger gardeners may not know is that coleus is a very frugal plant. From one coleus, you can get enough plants to keep your house and garden going for years. You can get enough plants to sell if you're so inclined. They root very easily. (Of course, I wouldn't know this either, younger gardener that I am, if not for Grammy and my extraordinary memory.)

Fill up a glass of water with cuttings, keep refreshing the water, and in a couple of weeks, there'll be lots of roots—baby plants ready to pot up. Enjoy them in the house all winter, and take more cuttings next spring to bed out, plant out in containers, or sell at a yard sale or flea-market table.

I find it better to take slips (cuttings) than to bring outdoor plants and soil inside in the fall, because you can bring in all kinds of unwanted critters. Be careful with cut flowers too. When I was a hotel gardener, I always sprayed the garden bouquets well with an organic soap spray, and let them sit for a few hours before placing them on the tables. Even so I remember one hair-raising earwiggy occasion—just before the guests sat down, thank goodness.

Another common house plant that will reward you with cuttings, and that I've seen more of lately, is German ivy. Back in the days before I became a serial house-plant killer, German ivy was one of my favourites. Ivies were very popular in Victorian homes, as were ferns, and you can buy them now as garden centre annuals a lot cheaper than you could get them a few years back as house plants.

I want you to know I wasn't always, and am not now, a serial killer of house plants. As a new homemaker years ago, I went through quite a love affair with house plants. Of course I went head over heels and couldn't get enough of them, and ended up with banks of them all over the house. Then I got fed up because they were too demanding, and well, the rest isn't pretty.

I wouldn't be thinking of them now but for the increasing numbers of crossovers from the house to the garden. Seeing the "coolie" from my grandmother's parlour as the star attraction in a modern steel planter is sort of like seeing Maurice Chevalier in a rap band; interesting and certainly worth remarking on.

Next week, I'm going to visit my Stephenville garden again, which was a lot friendlier to me than my new garden is. I know I'm being a whiner, but if I ever buy another house, I'll check out the soil first. You wouldn't pay as much for a house with a poor foundation, so soil from hell should be worth a thousand or two off the asking price!

AUGUST

The Path Less Travelled

I THINK I NEED TO KEEP MORE GARDENING PHILOSOPHY in mind when it comes to men. Some are definite weeds. I discovered on my trip to Stephenville that Tall-and-Handsome is like a biennial, a Canterbury Bell maybe; very showy, but high maintenance, and not always around when you want him.

There's another chap, however, who could be a calendula. Not the most flamboyant flower in the garden, but attractive in a quiet way, and easy to get along with. Always cheerful and very versatile. A safe choice if you could have only one flower in your garden and value dependability. A person could grow to love and rely on calendulas without even realizing it. They're like that.

God, I'm in bad shape this week, so I went to see my friend Janine for some girl talk about the species encountered on my path in life.

There she was with a new path of her own but literally. It runs in a no-nonsense straight line from the front door to the road, is wide and imposing, and is made out of expensive pavers. It's the silliest thing I have ever seen.

Janine has been in the same house for years. Even with three boys, there is no sign that anyone has ever taken that route to the street. Everyone comes up the driveway and across the grass to the steps. A

well-worn track in the lawn testifies to that fact. "Janine," I said, "what made you decide to put that path in?"

"That should be obvious," she answered, with a look that clearly questioned my credentials as a gardening columnist. "Look at that worn spot from everyone taking a short cut from the driveway. I should have had a path years ago."

Emboldened by my gin and tonic and feeling somewhat piqued that we weren't talking about *my* life's path problems, I ventured, "But why didn't you put the new path where the old path has been worn?"

"Because from the street, you wouldn't really see how nice it looks," she explained patiently, as if to a child.

"Has anyone used it yet?" I asked bravely.

"I use it," she said. "The others will get used to it gradually, especially once I fill in that bare spot."

There seemed no point in telling her that professional landscapers recommend waiting a year to put in paths to see what natural foot-traffic patterns develop. Nobody is ever going to get out of their car in the driveway and walk around to the new path. If she fills in the worn spot with a flower bed and a fountain and a partridge in a pear tree, people will walk around it and make a new path. Only a fence will stop the stream of feet between the driveway and the house, because that is the natural flow of things.

I didn't point out that with the money she spent on that long lonely path she could have done the sensible path of everyone's choice with the expensive pavers, and had enough money left to make her whole garden look nice from the street. I could have, but I didn't. It's her garden, and if she wants to pave the works and paint it green, it's her business. Janine enjoys looking at that path as much as I enjoy looking at a rambling rose.

But with garden paths as with life paths, some routes do make more sense than others.

My Spirit Needs Flowers

I KNOW WHY I DON'T HAVE CUTTING FLOWERS this year. But to tell you the truth, at least once every year, I end up wishing I had planted more cutting flowers. Sometimes I'm just one step away from raiding other people's gardens!

Especially right now. Dad is very sick, and the family is here. A lot of time is being spent in the hospital. I have even less interest than usual in routine housekeeping. I think, "I must straighten away the living room," at least two or three times a day. Then I wander into the kitchen and think the same thing.

And, rationally or not, I think if I had lovely sprawling bouquets of flowers in every room, I'd be much more motivated.

You just can't put a lovingly arranged bunch of flowers down in the middle of a mess. Right away I would have to scurry about, making the surroundings worthy. Even a jelly glass of wildflowers deserves more respect than dusty tabletops and last week's newspapers.

My favourite bouquets are casual and loose. The admirer who would send me a stiff florist's "arrangement" would nip any possible romance in the bud, so to speak. In fact, I almost never take buds from the garden, breaking, I know, one of the rules of making cut flowers last as long as possible. I'd rather enjoy them in the garden until they're fully open, and then bring them inside for their last glory. One of my garden favourites, the venerable day lily, isn't any good at all for cutting. It's called day lily for a reason; the blooms, although there are lots of them, last only a day (unless they've come up with new hybrids I don't know about yet).

Full-blown roses, dropping petals, will please my senses every time over tight young buds with little experience in sun or wind. And lest you think this is somehow symbolic of my own advancing state of bloom, let me point out that I have always been drawn to ripeness in flowers.

I suppose one reason I never seem to end up with enough cutting flowers is because I'm not fond of many of the traditional best ones. Stiffness of stem and uniformity of petal doesn't appeal to me. There are exceptions, like coneflowers, but it seems a sin to take them away from the birds.

Take dahlias, for example, considered by many to be one of the finest cutting flowers. My mother grew scads of them: Pompom, Spider, Dinner Plate, the works. They have a wonderful range of colours and sizes, and last a long time in water. I don't relate to dahlias at all, even though we're well acquainted; I helped my mother dig, divide, and label them each fall. But if dahlias were people we would never be close friends. It's the way their petals are so orderly and symmetrical that puts me off. I can't help feeling that they're a little smug, like those girls back in high school whose hair always flipped just right, or the woman across the street who always has her clothes hung out first. I hope I don't offend all the dahlia lovers out there; they are wonderful flowers, just not my type.

Soon I will have to choose our goodbye flowers for my wonderful father. Right now I can't decide which ones suit his personality, but I will. It's important to me, even though I know he'd laugh at the thought. "What about a cabbage, my darling?" he'd joke. "That's good enough for me."

I want to find a wonderful, tough, unpretentious flower with a zest for life. Only then will it be good enough for him!

Don't Forget Props

I'VE ALREADY CONFESSED A WEAKNESS for garden gadgets and stuff. Arguably, it could be because having good garden stuff around reinforces the illusion of being a good gardener. An attractive potting bench with stacks of clay pots, a mound of dark soil and a container or two of annuals may well distract from the fact that the garden is less than it might be. A tiller screams serious gardener. And a composter or a garden cart commands tremendous respect from non-gardeners.

Janine has that principal figured out. All summer her garden has been pretty blah. (There's only so much appeal to a new walkway). This week I saw her outside a garden centre, loading a new wheelbarrow, potting soil, and what seemed like dozens of flats of tired bedding plants into the back of her car. "For my front garden," she explained. "It was all on sale." I refrained from remarking that it was kind of late to be putting annuals in. Better late than never is my philosophy.

Then I drove by her house and there, at the front of her new walk, angled prettily, was the wheelbarrow, mounded high with a mass of colour. She put in a bunch of rocks (leftover from making the new walkway), dumped in the soil, and squeezed in every one of those less than prime annuals. Massed together they looked great. No one will really notice anymore how boring the rest of her garden is. Everyone will remember the wheelbarrow, and Janine is now considered a gardener. Now wouldn't that tick you off!

But I digress from gadgets. While a compost tumbler is tops on my list, I've seen two other garden gizmos lately, in a magazine, that I really want. One is a very small shredder. I've wanted a shredder forever, but they always seem too big and intimidating, not to mention expensive. Then I saw this cute little yellow one: "Powerful enough to cut through branches one inch thick." The name on it wasn't clear, but it looked like "Gloria Euro 1400." Still not in my price range at $299 US, but moving in the right direction.

I really really want this second one: "Can o' Worms," even though I don't think it would replace a tumbler. It's a layered container that lets worms compost all your kitchen scraps: "As worms digest each layer they move up to the next level, leaving behind valuable castings to enrich your soil."

I choose not to dwell on the origin of the "valuable castings." After all, I handle manure without squeamishness. I just think this is such a marvellous way to let worms do all the work. The picture in the magazine was the same size as the picture of the spiked sandals that you strap on to aerate your grass, so it's hard to judge its size. I'd guess around two feet high and maybe eighteen inches in diameter, with three layers and a cover. I don't know if the worms come with it or not, but if they don't, they should. At $119, it's not completely out of my reach, especially if I don't have to supply the worms.

Let's get back to the spiked sandals. At fourteen US dollars, they're more likely to be what I'll get as a gift sometime, so let's get it straight right now. I don't want them! I don't like grass well enough to walk around on it strapped to a pair of boards with two-inch nails protruding from the bottom. And what I want to know is how you can just "stroll" as they say in the ad, when you're being nailed to the grass with every step?

That's the kind of gadget that would reinforce a body's reputation as an eccentric—and that kind of reinforcement I can do without!

Of Berms and Mountains

I DROVE BY A PLACE THE OTHER DAY WHERE the gardener is obviously made of stronger stuff than I am. I knew the people in the house had just moved in during the spring, and there, where once only scrubby grass had stood, was a nice big square bed, full of things that I couldn't identify from the road, but which certainly looked impressive. The reason I give this unknown gardener credit for being of stronger stuff than I, is the huge pile of rocks to the side of the bed. It almost inspired me to come home and try digging just one more time. Especially since I'm off to Spain next month, and know from experience that hours of hard gardening can make a difference in your toreador pants.

The first summer I gardened professionally, I lost thirty-five pounds. Of course, that was being at it at least eight hours a day. It was a wonderful way to make a living; getting paid for doing something I loved doing, plus saving on Weight-Watchers' fees. Unfortunately I can't afford to put in those kinds of hours when I'm not getting paid for them, plus that was almost fifteen years ago, and I was a leaner, meaner machine to start with.

No, I think I'll lie down until the digging feeling goes away, stick with my plan of making raised beds. But what also sticks in my mind is that pile of rocks. Picture me going up and knocking on the door and asking these unsuspecting people if they were "suffering the heartbreak of heavy rocks" and then going on to tell them about the "berm-ease cure."

I really wanted to do it, but I didn't. Janine keeps warning me about getting arrested or committed, shot for trespassing, or bitten by a guard dog. Even though I keep reminding her that we're in Newfoundland, not New York, I do concede that not everyone might be delighted with a stranger on their steps raving about berms.

A berm is a man-made mound. It can take any shape you want it to. Berms are great for making flat gardens interesting, cutting down on street

noise, or discouraging foot traffic across a space. A high one will sig-
nificantly raise the level of plant material, giving you more privacy or
blocking out something you don't want to see. All very nice, but my
mind working the way it does, the really exciting thing about making
a berm is the silk-purse/sow's-ear factor.

You have an ugly, heavy pile of rocks, or a mess of broken concrete,
and other construction debris. Instead of worrying about how to get
rid of it, mound it to suit your site, dump a load or two of topsoil on
it, and a berm is born. How much soil you need depends on what you
want to plant on it.

Like any offspring, there are endless ways it can turn out, depending on you, the parent. Oh yes, there's always the potential for guilt.
If you put bad stuff into it, toxic waste like oil drums for example, you
won't get good stuff out of it. If you use big organic matter, like tree
stumps, eventually it will decay and you'll have a lot of settling. But
excavation rubble, plain old rocks, or even concrete will give it a good
solid base, and you can make something really interesting.

Don't you poor gardeners with rock-free soil and no construction
debris around your house feel deprived? Never mind, odd as it may
sound, there are some people who aren't as affectionate towards
berms as I am. They'll not only share their rubble, they may actually
allow you to come and take what you want. Otherwise, you can always
order a load or two of clean fill.

But that's not nearly as satisfying as making use of your own rocks.
Of course, in my case, I could end up with a mountain or a mole hill.

SEPTEMBER

The Veranda Was Unfolding as It Should

I THINK I DID A PRETTY GOOD JOB of turning my veranda into an extension of my living space. The wicker tables and chairs, the rocking chairs, a round straw mat, even a giant crib-board-cum-table all turned out to be very inviting. The begonias I planted in the spring came along nicely, with gorgeous big blooms, as did the huge fuchsias I picked up for a song (they should be at their peak right about now). Even the house plants that I moved outdoors for the summer seemed to love it.

Then I went away for a few weeks, and left Baby Sister and Brother-in-Law to do the watering and feed the cats. That went well I guess, until Baby Sister decided to join me for the last week, and B-i-L was left in charge.

All I can say is, thank goodness cats are pretty good at looking after themselves. They came through unscathed.

My poor plants were looking woebegone when I got back, but I figured a good soaking in a tub of water was all they needed to perk them up. Not so. I guess once they've gone too far, there's no bringing them back. Not only that, but the begonias have broken out in mildew.

These are the times when I am a tad ashamed. A really good gardener would have whipped out the sulphur powder as soon as the first whitish signs appeared. I thought, "Oh I must pick up some sulphur powder," and kept forgetting to do it. I know you're thinking, "she's too hard on herself, anyone could forget." You're sweet, but, let's face it: there are other elements to enjoying veranda life that I never forget to pick up. Now I'm going to have to get the begonias off the veranda altogether, because looking at them can really take the joy out of a gin and tonic, and they're hard to ignore.

Of course I knew my mistake when B-i-L told me over the phone that the big fern was looking great, so the problem couldn't be anything he was doing. Of course the big fern was looking great—it still is. In fact, it's been looking great for about fifteen years. I keep moving it around to wherever I need a little visual plant help. Even B-i-L couldn't do much damage to a silk fern!

Daughter #1 is back from her summer working (?) in Germany. She's decided to move into the old apartment in my basement. And why not; the price is right and there's a grocery store and laundromat right upstairs. She's in a flurry of picking out paint colours, and guess what she's counting on for part of her decor? My veranda stuff!

This is fine, and even somewhat flattering, because her friends have very chic apartments, but I've never been known to bring in the outdoor furniture until well after the first frost date.

Okay, I have been known to leave it out all winter, but I would never have done that with this nice stuff, which was really house furniture in a previous life anyway. So she'll have a very nice gardeny-looking place downstairs, which, if you read any decorating magazines at all, you'll know is all the style. People are bringing everything indoors: potting benches, trellises, even sections of picket fence to camouflage the fridge or turn into a headboard. She'll reclaim her houseplants, with only a few fatalities. (I managed to underwater the cactus!)

I'll help her decorate; I'll donate the veranda furniture. But she's not getting my Boston fern!

49

OCTOBER

Sometimes Bigger Is Better

HAVING PUT MY POOR BEGONIAS OUT OF THEIR MISERY, I find myself with empty containers. One of the things I have in common with Mama Nature is that I, too, abhor a vacuum. Remember, I've never seen an empty space I didn't want to fill. You'd think, with all the whining I've done about the garden this year, that I'd have enough sense to know when to quit. Instead, determined compulsive gardening masochist that I am, I'm heading out to the nursery once more.

I might find some potted chrysanthemums to fill my containers with colour for another couple of months. But even if I don't, it's bulb time. Already I have visions of pots of hyacinths lining my front steps, greeting me every day with heady perfume. I can see masses of tulips banked in the corner by the hammock, brilliant blue scilla among the English ivy.

This is not the time to point out to me that my visions are often the best part of my garden. To me, of all the acts of gardening, planting bulbs in the fall is the most profound. Burying bulbs in ground

165

that you know will soon be frozen and snow covered is an act of faith and optimism. Faith that the cycle of life will continue again in the spring. Optimism that, indeed, you'll be around to enjoy it.

Planting bulbs is actually a wonderful way to introduce toddlers to gardening. They're easier for little ones to handle than seeds, and sturdier than seedlings. Once they're planted there's nothing showing that tempts wee hands to pull them out of the ground. If you help them make their own little bed or mark the spot well, the children will remember in the spring, and will have learned all kinds of subliminal stuff about patience and miracles. Even if I lived in an area where munching squirrels were a problem, I'd have to find a way to plant bulbs. I'd be that weird lady salvaging mesh fruit baskets and all manner of wire containers from sidewalk garbage cans to protect my bulbs from marauders. I haven't seen a squirrel since I moved in here, so I'm not going to worry about that.

Actually, if we did have lots of squirrels around, there's a good chance I still wouldn't worry about it, but I might worry over the fact that I probably should be worrying about it and wasn't.

I'm not particularly fond of bulbs in beds. I do love them in containers, but naturalized bulbs are my favourite.

Naturalized simply refers to bulbs that are planted under trees or in the grass, and left to multiply naturally year after year. It sounds so simple, but there are a few little necessities, if you want them to really take hold and spread. The most important one is don't mow them down in the spring after they've stopped blooming. That slowly decaying foliage may not look like much to you, but through it, the bulb is gathering the nutrients it needs to bloom another year. Obviously this may not work well on a formal front lawn, which I suppose is exactly why I like it. I know I've told you this before but there's no harm in repeating it.

It's also a good idea to feed the bulbs in the fall. All you can really do with naturalized bulbs is scratch some good compost, or fertilizer, into the ground as best you can, and let the rains do the rest.

Then there is "making them look natural." The tried and true method is to simply toss them on the ground in handfuls and plant them where they fall. They don't really look right all higgledy-piggledy on the ground. You may get an urge to rearrange them. Resist it.

Even bulbs in beds are better planted in groups. Back in the days when I was a less tolerant gardener, I felt a little condescending whenever I saw a row of single tulips, lined up like tin soldiers marching off to battle. Now I think if it looks okay to you, do it. But maybe you could just try the grouping method. Purists recommend odd numbers of bulbs in each clump: five, seven, nine, whatever. I don't get too carried away with counting things, but I confess I actively scorn lines.

I also actively scorn paying more for anything than I have to, but with bulbs, get the best, because with bulbs, bigger is better.

But not always with other things.

50

End-of-Season Hysteria?

OCTOBER OF COURSE IS THE TIME TO BE THINKING about fall garden chores. I used to love fall garden chores: tidying up beds, digging up summer bulbs, planting fall bulbs, dividing stuff. Sunny fall days are a great time to be in the garden, because they're not too hot. Usually.

But right now, the weather is still so wonderful that my brain doesn't really believe it's October. I'm still in the "picking wild flowers" mode. I picked a gorgeous bouquet last week, asters and goldenrod, just there by the side of the path for the taking. They're still brightening my kitchen table, and Janine asked me what was the trick to making them last so long.

I wanted to sound really clever, but actually all I did was give them fresh water every day or so. I do know about adding stuff to the water; I just don't always get around to it.

We started talking about all the things we've heard of that are supposed to make cut flowers last longer. Not just the ones you pick yourself, but the bought ones you should start treating yourself to when there are none left to pick. "Sugar," said Janine, "or aspirin, or a few drops of bleach."

"You have to be more specific," I said knowledgably, "like two table-spoons of vinegar and three teaspoons of sugar to a quart of water."

"A half quart each of water and 7-Up, plus a half teaspoon of chlo-rine bleach," countered Janine.

"Make a solution of two tablespoons fresh lemon juice, one table-spoon sugar, and one-and-a-half teaspoons of bleach in a quart of water. One half cup of this added to the vase will feed the flowers and act as a mild fungicide," I intoned.

Of course she accused me of making it up to show off, and of course I dug out a book to prove I was doing no such thing. We also found out that a copper penny in the water will keep some flowers from opening too widely. Then we read that adding vodka to the water will make tulips stand up straight and last longer.

Now there's an interesting tip, I thought, for all those times you have left-over vodka and just don't know what to do with it. But, as Janine suggestively pointed out, maybe it doesn't just work on tulips. Therefore, it could be a very valuable tip. Now I ask you! I often won-der how people discover these tips. Was some woman given a drink that she only pretended to drink, but secretly poured into a vase of tulips? When the tulips were still standing long after Romeo wasn't, did some light dawn?

Remember that one for the spring, but how about this one for now? After you dig your carrots, put them in your automatic washer, with cold water, on the gentle cycle, then dry and store. When they say "dry" in a tip like this, I really think they should specify how, as one's mind could be forgiven for straying to the clothes line or the dryer. And why this should work only for carrots I have no idea. Why not potatoes? Maybe the skins would come off. Wouldn't the skins clog up the machine?

Here's another one. Store your summer bulbs in panty hose, hung in a dry place. If the thought of a nylon-clad lumpy bottom, legs, and feet hanging from your rafters doesn't put you off, you might be the type to try this next one: vacuum bugs off your beans, peppers, and tomatoes with the wand attachment of your vacuum cleaner.

Then try convincing your neighbours that you buy the vodka only for the flowers!

51

Thanksgiving Thoughts

MY MUSINGS, THIS YEAR, should have been called "Confessions of a Gin-and-Tonic Gardener." I mean, I do love the soil and growing things, "growing" in this case being an adjective, as much or more, than a verb. I love gardens and can never imagine myself being without one. My life's dream is of a cottage by the sea with an old-fashioned garden.

But my life's path is a meandering one, and this year the garden path has been downright rocky. I've felt more garden inadequacies this year than the rest of my life put together. Of course that's because I've experienced more garden inadequacies this year than ever before, and that includes when I was gardening on a windy ninth-floor balcony in downtown Halifax.

The reason I'm thinking about this so much this week is because I wanted to write a gardening Thanksgiving column. Then I realized that the thing I'm most thankful for in my garden this year is that the season is almost over and I won't have to think about it for a few months!

You have no idea how that realization depresses me. Not just depresses me, but horrifies me. I remember years when the Thanksgiving dinner was proudly served with vegetables from my own garden, and the table always, always, decorated from my own garden. Suddenly I'm overcome with loss, and am seized by the psychological whammy of less wanting more. So this year, when the best I can do is supply the parsley, I find myself not only aching for my dream garden by the sea, but visualizing a few geese wandering around, and hens, with maybe even a goat or two bleating in the background.

Obviously I'm going over the edge, having a major attack of gardening separation anxiety. This year, because of difficult soil and topography, and a generally "down" psyche, I convinced myself that planting a few shrubs and a few containers would satisfy me. Instead I feel worse than ever.

And, thinking about the garden at Thanksgiving makes me really miss my father, who lived with me before he died. Odd that I miss him now perhaps, because a gardener he wasn't. But before he became frail, he always helped me with the heavy work. In my very first garden we built stone steps and a path together. He used to remind me that he once won a prize for the biggest cabbage in the Newfoundland woods camps; never admitting that while he may have run the camp and gotten the credit, there was no way he was responsible for the size of that cabbage. Not the man who once helped me out in my garden centre, and told a customer that gladioli bulbs were onions. (I'm starting to repeat myself. Maybe it's good thing that this gardening year is almost over.)

I'm really sad that in this St. John's garden there is nothing that he helped me with, simply because he wasn't able to. The veranda, however, will continue to be home to the old glider rocker where he enjoyed his afternoon toddy, and to the handmade crib table that we used on calm warm days when I got tired of being skunked indoors.

The gardening season isn't totally over, but for me it is. I am anxious to put this unsettled year behind me and greet a new spring. My daughters are independent, and for the first time in my entire adult life I am alone with no one to look after but myself.

And so I've made another big decision. I'm going to get as close as I can, without moving again, to having the garden cottage of my dreams. Next year I'm going to rent out the big main house and renovate the old basement apartment to create a garden flat, just for me. Instead of being high up on the deck looking down at the garden, I'll have a Dutch door opening right into it. I'll be able to watch the birds first thing in the morning before I even get out of bed. I'll have a huge kitchen/great room with the cozy wood stove I've been missing, and a window seat, and a corner where I can write and enjoy both the garden and the fire. The apartment bathroom has an old claw-foot tub and with the right window I'll even be able to look out at the garden while I soak.

You can't imagine how much this decision has rejuvenated me and restored my spirit. My winter days will be spent planning the flat and the garden. My winter nights will be spent, as always, with the heat turned way down. Snuggled under a feather duvet and a fur blanket in the big iron and brass bed that was my father's when he was a child, I will dream of gardens past, and with the tip of my cold nose, try to catch the scent of the garden that will be.

Some Easy-Going Garden Friends and Why I Like Them

These are their common names. Most of these plants have dozens of varieties.

Shrubs

Burning bush: gorgeous fall colour.

Flowering quince: oriental looking, stunning in mid to late spring.

Forsythia: the branches covered with bright yellow flowers in early spring give me a lift.

Mock orange: wonderful scent, especially in vases.

Mugho pine: very hardy evergreen, good dark colour.

Pee Gee hydrangea: fall blooms that change colour and dry well.

Weigelas: easy and reliable summer bloomers.

Ground Covers

I like anything that lets me get rid of grass.

Ajuga:	easy to grow, can be stunning in the spring.
Cotoneasters:	evergreen, interesting textures and colours, plus nice berries.
Lamium:	good for shade, many attractive varieties.
Low-growing junipers:	evergreen, interesting textures and colours.
Periwinkle:	attractive dark leaves and bluish flowers, but a bit slow to establish.
Sweet woodruff:	good for shade, many attractive varieties.
Thyme:	good to look at, cook with, even walk on.

Perennials Good for Combining with Ground Covers

Day lily:	will forgive you almost anything.
Ribbon grass:	provides nice contrast.
Lungwort:	likes shade, pretty bell-shaped flowers in spring.

Perennials for Full Sun or Part Shade

Asiatic lily:	masses of blooms, many colours.
Black-eyed Susan:	love the golds and bronzes, volunteers.*
Calendula:	really an annual, but a wonderful volunteer.
Coreopsis:	cheerful, can be quite tall.**
Forget-me-not:	biennial varieties volunteer.
Geranium:	very reliable, don't confuse with the annual type.

Mallow:	tough, blooms all summer.
Peony:	can go for many years without needing dividing.
Purple coneflower:	unusual shape, long lasting, attracts birds.
Snow-in-summer:	greyish-green leaves, scented, easy, cascades.**

* Reseeds itself each year

** Can get out of control; watch where you put it

Perennials That Can Take More Shade

These aren't all personal favourites, but they are very useful.

Astilbe:	feathery-like blooms, soft colours.
Bee balm:	likes space, best planted alone in clumps.
Bleeding heart:	love this one, reminds me of Grandpa's garden.
Columbine:	can have some lovely colour combinations, volunteers.
Coralbells:	delicate-looking flowers borne above nice mounds.
Day lily:	here we go again, very versatile.
Hosta:	variegated varieties brighten up shady spots.
Lungwort:	ditto.
Monkshood:	really old fashioned, poisonous, makes no demands.
Primrose:	low growing, spring blooming, many colours.

Perennial Vines and Climbing Things

Vines give you so much for so little ground space.
These are the ones I've grown:

Bittersweet:	fat, fabulous orange and scarlet berries, needs a mate.
Honeysuckle:	wonderful scent.
Virginia creeper:	wonderful fall colour.

These are ones I plan to try:

Chinese wisteria:	huge blooms, and a twisty, gnarly trunk.
Clematis:	had no luck the first time, but worth another try.
Japanese hydrangea rosea:	hard to find, but looks worth the hunt.

Shrub Roses

David Austins:	hardy roses.
Explorer:	very hardy roses.
Frau Dagmar Hastrups:	(rugosa) single pink, low growing.
Hansa (rugosa):	red, keeps going even when abandoned, can grow to be eight feet tall.
Mordens:	ditto.

Climbing and Rambling Roses

Alberic Barbier: creamy white, considered very forgiving and can take shade.

Golden Showers: golden yellow, can take some shade.

Leverkusen: pale yellow, withstands exposed conditions.

Rambling Rector,
Kiftsgate: both creamy white and will cover old sheds, climb up trees, good hip display.

Zephirine Drouhin: thornless old favourite, can take some shade.

Two I planted last year that survived the winter with no protection:

America: seems to be quite vigorous.

Handel: gorgeous bicolour.

There are so many. Just remember the hybrid teas are usually the fussiest and the shrubs are usually the most forgiving.

Read, read, read.